One
with the
Sea

AN INSPIRING

RAGS-TO-RICHES SAGA

OF THE SON OF AN IRISH IMMIGRANT

To Bob,

Aug 11, 2013

We hope you enjoy
this story of a man
with Irish roots
who love of the sea
developed into an amazing
career.

Happy 80th,

Love,
Teresa and Ed

One
with the
Sea

AN INSPIRING

RAGS-TO-RICHES SAGA

OF THE SON OF AN IRISH IMMIGRANT

by

Richard Daniel O'Leary

Jetty House
an imprint of
Peter E. Randall Publisher
Portsmouth, New Hampshire
2011

ISBN 10: 0-9828236-5-7
ISBN 13: 978-0-9828236-5-1
Library of Congress control number: 2011922420

Published by:
Jetty House
Peter E. Randall Publisher
Box 4726
Portsmouth, NH 03802
www.perpublisher.com

Book Design: Grace Peirce

Permission granted by The Millay Society to reprint "Exiled" © 1922, 1950 by Edna St. Vincent Millay.

"Father and Son," by F. R. Higgins—from *The 39 Poems*. Selected and edited by R. Dardis Clarke. Published by the Bridge Press, Dublin.

Cover Photo:
Richard O'Leary on his Hinckley sailboat directing four of his *Spirit*-class passenger vessels in New York Harbor during the July 4, 1986, Statue of Liberty unveiling celebration.

This book is dedicated to my three sisters:

Arlene, Ethel, and Mary.

Contents

Introduction

I would guess that almost everyone experiences a few "up" and "down" days in their journey through life. One of my really down days was during the winter of 1943 when I was going on twelve years of age and living in Auburn, Maine.

Our family was living through the difficulties associated with being poor. We lived in one of the worst rentals of the many bad ones I had known. It was so bad that I would leave by a back door and climb a hill so people would not know I lived there. We had no heat at night so this meant sleeping more or less fully dressed and piling coats on the beds. Although we were never really hungry our diet left a good deal to be desired in terms of nutrition and appeal.

Although successful in school, I was not a confident or secure young boy. I was also ashamed of my personal clothing, which was not comparable to that worn by my schoolmates. I also suffered from severe facial acne. I found myself having difficulty making direct eye contact with people.

The war was still on and it was an unsettling period for everybody, and particularly for the O'Leary family.

I had managed to get a paper route delivering the *Lewiston Evening Journal*. I did not read newspapers but sometimes when the truck delivered them to me I would glance at the front page. On this particular day I noticed a headline and a story that said that it would be possible in the future to push a button and send powerful bombs across the ocean and blow up entire cities. This was shocking and frightening to me. My hard working father then worked for the city of Auburn building catch basins, another term for sewers. When I returned home from delivering the papers I learned that there had been an accident and that my father had broken his shoulder. Although I was never a pessimistic or really unhappy boy, life did not seem very promising to me on that day.

Forty-four years later, on May 1, 1987, I was in New York City. I was there to introduce a brand-new 600-passenger harbor cruise ship named the *Spirit of New York* to the city of New York. The ship was constructed and owned by Cruise International, a company located in Norfolk, Virginia, that I founded and eventually led for over thirty-four years.

It was a gala day, and certainly one of the most exciting days of my life. The ship was greeted by New York City fireboats spraying plumes of red, white, and blue water and by the United States Merchant Marine Academy trumpeters.

There were 600 guests for the inaugural luncheon cruise and another 600 for the inaugural dinner cruise that evening. The guests included many of the luminaries of the New York scene, including Alair Townsend, deputy mayor of New York, and David Rockefeller, chairman of the New York Chamber of Commerce. We sailed with many high-level dignitaries, including seven presidents of cruise ship companies.

Prior to performing the traditional bottle-breaking ceremony, Deputy Mayor Townsend spoke to the crowd. Included in her remarks was the following:

"Welcome home, Dick. We are fortunate to have such a beautiful new ship from which to view one of the world's greatest vistas. I have little doubt this ship is going to be one of New York City's spectacular star attractions!"

I responded by saying:

"We have been doing business in most other major East Coast cities with both Ocean Cruise vessels and our own *Spirit* harbor vessels and we do quite an audacious thing. For the last six years, we have had a New York Broadway revue on each of our vessels. You will see that show soon and hear a song about New York. The words say: 'If I can make it there, I'll make it anywhere.' I wish you to know that we have reversed that process. We have made it almost everywhere else and I am here to tell you today that we are now coming to make it in New York."

That evening, my wife, Barbara, and I had a refreshing sleep in the Plaza Hotel. We awakened the next day to see a picture of the *Spirit of New York* on the front page of the business section of the *New York Times*.

And the *Spirit* did indeed make it in New York. She had record sales the first year. She also served as the site of the New York Maritime Day celebration and is still sailing to this day.

Our company continued to grow rapidly in its various divisions and the *Spirit* fleet expanded to Chicago and the West Coast.

While sitting on the dais on that very "up" day, I remember having a flashback and thinking about some of the "down" days of my youth. It was fleeting, but it reminded me how fortunate I had been and how good life had been to me.

Obviously, the two days I have chosen to mention illustrate the dramatic changes that occurred in my life. It is these changes that are the subject matter of this memoir. I am sure there are many reasons why these changes happened to me. I would include God and the fact that I was born in America, which truly is a land of opportunity.

A person who played a very large role in my life was my father. He was less fortunate than me and he was not born in America.

On May 27, 1889, he was born in a stone, dirt-floor farmhouse in a small townland called Derryvahalla, near Bantry Bay, County Cork, Ireland. He was one of nine children born of the union of Cornelius O'Leary and Mary Harrigan. His siblings had the common names of Julia and John, as well as unlikely names such as Cornelius, Flurry, and Jeremiah.

This boy lived the life of a typical Irish youth of that time: poverty and hard manual labor mixed with an acceptance of life as it happens to you. In the Irish tradition, he fatalistically accepted the vicissitudes of that life as the natural order of things.

The sons of an Irish family in those days were generally forced to leave one by one as they came of age. In 1908, at the age of nineteen, Daniel Cornelius O'Leary left his home, family, and country and sailed to America.

At first I was planning to title this book *Son of Danny Boy* and relate it to the song "Danny Boy." His story plays an important part in my life and thus in this memoir. But as I wrote, I realized that my love for the sea was the driving force behind most facets of my life. Thus, I somewhat reluctantly changed the title to *One with the Sea*, which I think is more appropriate and better ties together the different aspects of my life that I write about.

The story begins with a sea voyage: the crossing of the Atlantic Ocean by my father in search of a new beginning in America. The life he eventually lived included a family of which I was the only son. Ironically, I later crossed those same waters on ships hundreds of times. It's also on the shore of that same ocean where I discovered my deep fascination with the sea. All of the important chapters and successes of my own life have been directly or indirectly inspired by that experience. As I write this, about one hundred years after his crossing, I'm sitting in our Ogunquit, Maine, home next to a window with a view of the wide-open Atlantic.

I have enjoyed, in full measure, a remarkable life that I have always taken for granted as the luck of the Irish. Over the decades, a number of people have said to me, "There must be a book in you." This was a notion I thoroughly rejected, despite the fact that my very talented eldest daughter, Lauren, has been working on a book for about two years.

Although I know I'm a garrulous storyteller, I accepted it as part of being Irish. I never considered myself a writer except for business letters and imposed academic writing.

Because of the persistence of a few friends who insisted I had a story to tell, I've reluctantly agreed to try. Among those friends are Jim Denton, now the publisher and editor of *World Affairs* journal, and Walter Galliford, a very scholarly gentleman. The words spoken by Mayor Paul Fraim, of Norfolk, Virginia, at my retirement party also helped spark some interest in writing.

I think it was when I heard the word "memoir" and then contemplated my newly acquired free time that the idea first appealed to me.

I retired from my company in July 2005, after nearly thirty-five years. My wife, Barbara, along with personnel from our advertising department, created a very beautiful book of letters from good friends and wonderful pictures. I've taken the liberty of including some of these to help me tell this story.

I have written this with a somewhat thematic approach rather than a strict chronology of events. I have done my best to accurately report what has transpired in my life, but sometimes I had to rely only on my own memory, and if there are any errors, they are mine.

Richard Daniel O'Leary

Above: View of the author's home in Ogunquit. Below: View of Atlantic Ocean as seen from the O'Leary home in Ogunquit, Maine.

The Barrys of Derryvahalla, circa 1980.

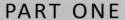

1

Life in Ireland
at the Turn of the
Nineteenth Century

 any of the details contained in this chapter became available to me because of my love for and curiosity about my father and the early part of his life. After I had enjoyed some semblance of success, I wanted to know more about this man whom I loved so intensely.

In 1990 my wife, Barbara, and I went on a golf cruise to Ireland and Scotland, which is surprising because I'm one of the world's worst golfers. Barbara, my soul mate, came back from the ship's beauty salon and told me she had met a young woman who lived in Derryvahalla. This was a serendipitous event for me. Her name was Murnone, and she was born and currently lived in one of the few houses in the very same, very small bit of Ireland that my father came from.

I met with her and she explained the concept of Irish oral history as it has passed down through the years. Because of her, I commissioned Jerome Daly, an oral historian, to investigate my family history. I was astonished at what he produced in facts as well as documents, such as my father's birth certificate and copies of the censuses of 1890, 1900, and 1910.

My wife and I have been to Ireland eight or so times. We have visited with the Barrys, the present occupants of the O'Leary land. Two of my daughters

RDO in front of his father's home in Derryvahalla, 1980.

have also visited. We tried, unsuccessfully, to bring one of the Barrys' sons to our summer home in Maine for a visit.

I remember the first day I set eyes on Derryvahalla. It was from a distance and I was looking down on it from the direction of Glengarriff. The area, with its lush green hills near the lovely waters of Bantry Bay, is magical, and reminds me of parts of my native state, Maine. The resemblance is remarkable.

The land itself isn't much, enough for a few houses. I'm guessing that it's three or four miles square. It climbs up the side of a hill or low mountain. It has some of the multi-greens of Ireland, and low, gray-stone buildings. It's quite picturesque and, in a strange way, very beautiful.

Most of the original stone houses are now in disuse. It's when you get up close and look in them that you sense how startlingly different life was for these people from anything we know today. Dirt floors, tiny rooms, stone fireplaces, large families, animals mostly roaming free: all are indicators of another era.

Yet there is something almost mystical about it. A few years ago, my daughter Leslie was visiting Derryvahalla with her husband, Steve. After looking around a bit, Steve turned to her and said, "Why did he ever leave here?" The answer is that he had no choice.

The following is one of a number of letters from Mr. Daly.

> LISHEENS
> OVENS
> CO. CORK
> IRELAND
> 23-12-1993
> Tel 021 871418

Dear Richard,

Many thanks for your letter and cheque which I received this week. I am really delighted to see that the son of a Derryvahalla emigrant has done so fantastically well in the United States.

Don't worry about the previous material which was mislaid, I will replace it all when the government offices open again after Christmas. I also hope to get a birth certificate for your father and maybe a death certificate for your paternal grandfather, Cornelius.

Regarding a possible trip to Ireland by yourself, I would be only too pleased to meet you. We have a house in Schull, which is occupied only during the summer months and you and your wife, and members of your family, if they are interested, are welcome to the use of it while you are here. It is 20 minutes' drive from Derryvahalla and would be a nice base to use while traveling around meeting some of your relations, meeting some old-timers and visiting your grandparents' grave, etc. Most of the people around here are in farming and a suitable time for visiting them would be from mid-May to start of June. At this time the planting is completed and they are more leisurely. If you were to fly into Shannon and hire a car there you would be a free agent.

I would take a few days off work and introduce you to some interesting places and people and make your visit an enjoyable one. If this idea appeals to you, you can let me know and the details regarding where to get the key, etc., will be worked out in advance of your trip. The world soccer championships finals are on in the USA this year, which should be a boost for your travel business. I will write again in about 3 weeks. In the meantime, I wish you all a happy new year.

Jerome Daly

I think Mr. Daly's work presents a good historical view of life in Derryvahalla, but I have a few firsthand answers to my questions that were relayed to me by my father.

When I asked how long he went to school, he would answer, I think facetiously, "two or three days." In my youth he still couldn't read or write, but he later became a good reader.

He once told me of putting a pail of water in the barn on New Year's Eve and the whole family going out at midnight to see if it had turned to wine.

When I inquired what he did for pleasure, he would describe Saturday trips either on foot or by horse and cart to Skibbereen, a seaside resort fifteen miles away.

In my father's time, the sons of an Irish family were forced to leave home and they generally depended on money for the trip from those who had preceded them. The tradition was to hold a big family party the night before one of the sons left for America. He would have to travel to Queenstown, now known as Cobh (Harbor of Tears), to board the ship. One of the last sights he would behold was the spire of the beautiful Catholic church there. Certainly most of these young men had to know they would never see their families again. Much has been written about the horrible conditions during these transatlantic voyages, when passengers usually endured cramped, filthy quarters; a month of seasickness; poor food; and boredom.

My father's ship docked in Philadelphia in 1908 rather than in New York, where most docked. When I asked him how he liked the sea trip, he said it was wonderful. He said he played a lot of tug-of-war and that his side always won. I knew something about sea voyages and knew it must have been summer. They also must have had very good weather, which is rare in the North Atlantic.

I later crossed these same waters hundreds of times as a navigation officer on the SS *United States*, at that time the greatest and fastest liner in the world. During those years he would be at home worrying and waiting for my calls.

LISHEENS
OVENS
CO. CORK
6-2-1995
started (Feb. 6th 1995)
completed 13th Feb.

Dear Richard,

I hope these contents will excuse my long delay in responding. They confirm that the oral tradition is correct. I had said in my last letter that your grandfather, Cornelius, was a fiddle player and performed at all local functions and occasions such as parties for people going off to America.

As can be seen from the papers enclosed the Learys were in Derryvahalla 150 years ago. Prior to that they were in the Borlin area. Some distant relatives of yours still live there. Your branch of the Learys was known as the Leary GLANNYS. This was to distinguish them from other unrelated Leary families. GLANNY comes from the Irish language word GLEN, and about 10 years ago the Leary clan had a big gathering in a glen near Ballingeary, which is supposed to be the start of the Leary settlement in west Co. Cork several hundred years ago.

I notice even today after perhaps 10 or 12 generations, the names CON, TIM, and MICHAEL are still very plentiful anywhere there is a family of Learys.

Your grandmother was a widow for about the last 25 years of her life. The other Leary family also had a widow as head of house.

Both your grandmother and the other Mrs. Leary were known by their original names. Mary Horgan was your grandmother and Mary Murphy was the other Leary widow.

At that time, it was usual for the eldest son to inherit the farm but he would not get married until all the younger members of the family were gone. Then at about the age of maybe 45, he would marry a woman of 20. These women tended to outlive their husbands but widowhood did not trouble them as long as they had a farm. This was seen as the ultimate security.

Your grandmother and grandfather, your uncles and aunts are all buried in the Leary flat in KILMOCOMOGUE on the east side of Bantry. They were born, reared, and died within a 10-mile radius of Bantry.

The grave does not have a headstone but one of your relations has a plaque on the boundary wall of the cemetery.

See how the love of music broke out again in the Leary clan.

They were and still are noted as very industrious and hardworking.

Your father, Daniel, worked for a farmer named O'Sullivan before going to America. This place is still occupied by Sullivans and is about one mile from his home place in Derryvahalla.

By the way, you will notice the different spellings of Derryvahalla, and your grandmother's name, Mary HORGAN, or HORRIGAN, or HORIGAN.

Your father stayed in the house where he worked even though it was less than a mile. No public lighting in Derryvahalla!

He was waiting for older members of his family who had immigrated to America to send him the fare for the ticket. This must have taken a year or more and he was beginning to despair of it ever coming. He was constantly watching the postman, who at that time used to deliver three days a week. The ticket arrived eventually to where he worked, he knew the postman brought a letter, but the farmer did not give it to him until evening time. If he got it in the morning there would be a danger that no more work would be done that day.

I believe your grandfather, Cornelius, may have had brothers and sisters in America before your father, Daniel, went out. He certainly had relations there and it may have been from this source your father got the ticket. He would not have much savings himself, as his wages would have been about $1 per week. He would have given perhaps half of this each week to his mother to help support the rest of the family. There was tremendous family and clan loyalty in Ireland at that time. It is still there but now very much diminished.

Now to the papers copied from the government offices. By the way, it amazes me that there existed in Ireland, 150 years ago, an administration that was able to record all households in the country and map every field and roadway. This was done when very few people were able to read and write. It was at the time of your father's birth that schooling became popular. Before that, only three or four people in Derryvahalla out of a population of about 50 were able to read and write. Note, your father and his family are given the occupation "scholar" in the 1901 census.

The most interesting sheet enclosed here is, I think, your father's birth certificate.

The 1901 census sheet is a poor photocopy but your father's name can be clearly seen. Your grandparents were both able to speak Irish and English. The Irish language would have been their natural tongue and the one they grew up with. They probably learned English from their children.

The valuation of tenements dated March 1853 is in fact the first tax imposed in Ireland. Each household had to pay the amount levied every year at that time: £1 = about $5. You can see that the bill was huge for the time. It was passed by the British Parliament, which ruled Ireland at the time. The idea was that Irish property would have to pay for Irish property. The country was in a very poor state after the famine of the 1840s. In 1841 there were 100 people in 16 houses in Derryvahalla. By 1851, there were only 43 people in 6 houses. Today there are 6 houses and 20 people.

I have ringed Jeremiah Leary in the valuation of tenements for Derryvahalla. He was Cornelius' father, your great-grandfather. That man divided his farm between two of his sons and that is how the two O'Leary families came to be in Derryvahalla.

I have also ringed Denis Horigan in the valuation of tenements, Parish of Gahreegh, Glonatnow. Your grandfather, Cornelius, married Denis Horigan's daughter, Mary, so Denis is another of your great-grandfathers.

Relations of yours in Ireland and England

MR. JERRY MAHONY SEHANES DRIMOLEAGUE CO. CORK, IRELAND TEL 028 31380	Your father had a sister, Julia, and this is her son, your first cousin. Julie died young and is buried with her parents in Kilmocomogue.
BERNIE LEARY, GARAGE PROPRIETOR BANTRY CO. CORK	
JERRY O'LEARY 31 DYKE STREET LIVERPOOL 6 ENGLAND 2NX TEL 512 60 4287 (Your code goes before this)	This Jerry was reared by his aunt and went to England as a young adult. He did not join the others and met his mother only a few times. Wife's name is Vera. He is your Uncle Florrie's son, your first cousin.

As I said earlier, Florrie died at about the age of 50. His widow, Jeanie, remarried. This man's name was Don Connolly and the following are two of her children. I think they would have contact with their step-sisters and stepbrothers. They are all in England.

CON & RENE CONNOLLY 5 BARNFIELD HIGHCLIFFE ESTATE WICKFORD ESSEX 5511.8 HP ENGLAND	Con's son is named Tim and his wife is Marcella.
Con's sister is BID MARRIED TO MAURICE HICK 69 BAWDSTY AVE NEWBURY PARK ILFORD ESSEX 1G2 7TN ENGLAND TEL (I think) 590 8552	

All this information should keep you going for some time, Richard. You might consider photocopying some of it in case it gets mislaid.

I wish you all the best for the present.

Yours faithfully,

Jerome Daly

P.S. I believe that the Murnone girl you met on the ship is a distant relation of yours.

Indeed it did keep me going for years, and the suggestion to photocopy the material is because I mislaid his previous mailing.

My father's birth certificate.

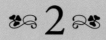

2

The
Missing Years

here's a gap of about twelve years about which my knowledge of my father's activities is scant. This period is from 1908 until 1920.

On a visit to see me in Norfolk, Virginia, my father told me he was interned for a while during World War I because he was an alien from a neutral country. Where he had this experience is now known as Norfolk International Terminal, and I was at one time in charge of the operation and development of this facility.

After his arrival in Philadelphia, my father somehow made his way to New York. This may have been motivated by a desire to find some of his family who had preceded him. I know this because he told me about a cousin named Dennis McCarthy. Mr. McCarthy and his family actually visited us many years later in Maine. He also spoke of an uncle who was a New York City detective. Years later, when I was a young boy, that uncle was murdered and thrown into the East River. My father took the train to New York to attend his funeral. It turned out to be an eventful trip. My father traded seats with someone in order to be able to play

My parents.

poker. Then the train crashed and the man who had switched seats with him was killed.

My father's first job in America was as a gardener at Sailor's Snug Harbor, on Staten Island, New York. It was a rest home for old sailors, and I have visited the area.

It seems from there he went to Boston and worked for some time as a longshoreman. The stories of how the Irish were treated in Boston are well documented. He was known as a greenhorn and was always among the last picked, if at all, for the worst jobs at the "shape-ups" on the Charleston waterfront. (He pronounced it "Charl-less-town.") He told me that the few jobs he got were on grain ships: the men went down into the holds and shoveled the grain by hand, wearing only handkerchiefs to protect them from the grain dust–filled air. He suffered from asthma for much of the rest of his adulthood. His social life consisted of Saturday-night trips to the Boston Common to drink beer.

I loved hearing about a job he had on a farm in Arlington, now a suburb of Boston. He used to drive a horse with a cart full of vegetables to the Boston outdoor market, which still exists. He was always bragging that the horse knew the way so he had nothing to do.

Daniel Cornelius O'Leary and Ruth Florence O'Leary.

He then went to the woods of Vermont to hand-cut trees, which is back-breaking work. He joked to me that everyone thought he was there to cut wood, but he was there to play poker at night and take their money.

He was in his early thirties at the time, had never married, and still practiced the Catholic faith. It is here that his life took a stunning turn that would transform the rest of his days. He accepted an invitation to go home for a weekend with one of the other woodcutters, a man named Guy Holly. How they traveled from Vermont to Kingfield, Maine, is beyond me. But I do know, because of a lot of family verification, that there he found Mr. Holly's wife, who was pregnant, and her four-year-old daughter. I know nothing of the actual details of that family, of course, but I have heard, through mine, that Mr. Holly, although a good person, had taken to drink and pushed his wife down the stairs.

Whatever happened, it seems my father ended up taking her away, and he married her in St. Johnsbury, Vermont. That woman was my mother. My father loved her fiercely for the rest of his life. "Loved her" is an understatement—he was utterly devoted to her.

Her maiden name was Ruth Florence Cook. Her mother emigrated from a town three miles from Derryvahalla. I was never clear about her father and never met him. I believe he drowned, and as a child I heard rumors of suicide. They had lived in upstate New York, and my grandmother lived with us for short periods when I was a boy.

Ruth Cook became Mrs. Guy Holly, and lived in Farmington and Kingfield, Maine. The couple had a child named Arlene, who was about four years old when my father met my mother. That little girl became one of my two half sisters, and I

RDO with sister, Mary Anne.

loved both of them dearly. She stayed with her father and graduated from Kingfield High School.

My mother moved to Auburn, Maine, with my father, where she had her second child. That child was my beloved half sister/half mother, Ethel. She lived with us for some twenty years. She wasn't as lucky as I was and had to go to work at about age fifteen to contribute to the family's income. At first she worked at a difficult, physical job in a shoe-manufacturing company. Then she was employed in a variety of jobs until her death at the age of eighty-three. This beloved example of goodness was a millionaire when she died.

When she was ten I came along, on June 16, 1932. Born in Central Maine General Hospital, I weighed in at ten pounds, ten ounces, the largest baby born there until that time. My parents told me everyone in the hospital called me Jack

Dempsey, after the famous boxer, mainly because I was the biggest and loudest baby in the ward. My mother was thirty-five and my father was forty-four, a typical age in those days for an Irishman to have his first child.

Four years later his second child, my sister Mary Anne, was born in the same hospital. This completes our family unit: my father, my mother, my half sister Ethel, and my sister, Mary. My half sister Arlene stayed with her father in Kingfield. We lived together until I was nineteen.

RDO with his two best friends.

3

Irish Childhood in Maine

Some years back Barbara and I were fortunate to be cruising on a grand new cruise ship named the *Millennium* in the Caribbean. We were guests of the owner, John Chandris, so we were in the owner's suite. The suite really is a small apartment with a private butler and a private dining room. It also has a balcony with a hot tub. We had just purchased two copies of Frank McCourt's masterpiece *Angela's Ashes*. This was the only time we had ever purchased two copies of a book or read two books at the same time. We both laughed and wept as we made our way through the book in that wonderful setting. It is ironic that we were ensconced in such luxury because much of the book takes place in conditions that were the polar opposite of what we were experiencing.

Frank McCourt begins the book with a description of his childhood, which in a word was miserable. I was amused by the fact that with his keen sense of humor and remarkable storytelling style he included in the middle of this description the insight that a happy childhood is hardly worth your while. He goes on to describe with vivid and moving verbiage life as a poor Irish Catholic child in Limerick, Ireland.

My childhood did not compare with that of Frank McCourt, but it was no walk in the park. My earliest memories are associated with poverty and terrible, unclean rentals. We moved more than twelve times in my first nineteen years, each place worse than the one before.

My father didn't have a steady job, but he worked almost all the time at difficult tasks. He was a human working machine whose only goal was to provide for his family. My mother, on the other hand, was less industrious. I remember her sitting and smoking cigarettes, eating raw oatmeal out of the box, and gossiping with neighbors.

We never were actually hungry, but I remember, near the end of the Depression, when I was about seven, accompanying my father and bringing home brown paper bags with packages of grain that were provided free by the government. We ate the cheapest foods available: fried pork, eggs, potatoes, mackerel,

RDO's father's citizenship certificate.

and tripe. Ironically tripe, which is the lining of a cow's stomach, was featured on the menu at New York City's famous 21 Club.

My mother's cooking abilities were on a par with her housekeeping, which was not noteworthy, but she was a good woman and she tried. Our diet left a lot to be desired. Of much greater importance, though, is that my father idolized this woman he called Susie rather than Ruth (and he was Nan rather than Dan).

Although I may appear a bit critical of my mother, I loved her. My father's love for her was powerful and unswerving; mine was not as intense. I remember that when I was six or seven years old, somehow it was arranged for her to go to Kennebunkport for a week to clean somebody's house. This was traditional for Irish women. She left in a chauffeur-driven limousine. I don't know how this came about, but I suspect it was because of Mrs. Monroe, the lady my father mowed lawns for. The point, though, is that my father and sisters and I missed her very, very much.

During this period a very important event happened in the life of our family. After much study, on March 8, 1939, my father became an American citizen. You can see from the certificate that he had learned to write a little. He was fifty years of age and I was seven. This was a time of great pride for our family.

One incident that has always stood out in my mind concerns pudding, which I loved. I would explain to my mother that all you had to do was empty the contents of the Jell-O box into two cups of milk. She would do that, but also add a number of other ingredients, such as flour, cornstarch, sugar, and eggs. When I took a bite, invariably I would get a mouthful of flour, but my father told her he liked it better that way.

We also used to go on blueberry-picking excursions, which I resisted to the extent that I could. We would bring home five-gallon pails of blueberries, and then the canning process began—washing the jars, boiling the fruit, and attempting to seal the jars with rubber gasket–like devices. The payoff in winter was usually disappointing, especially to me; most of the contents would have green mold on top: not good in a blueberry pie.

The custom in our home, as in lots of other families, was to heat water on the stove and take baths on Saturday evening. When I became a teenager, I began heating my own water on the stove, after cleaning the tub, two or three days a week. This was a source of some annoyance to my family; to this day I have a fastidious bent, and often shower twice a day.

In the early 1940s, my father got a steady job with the city of Auburn's highway department. This was comforting but did little to change our economic status. He also became a mason of sorts and, along with a small crew of men, dug and constructed a large percentage of the sewers in Auburn.

RDO at fifteen.

My first job was as a paperboy for the *Lewiston Evening Journal* (I was two years under the age to work there). I used the little money I made to try to improve my terrible clothes, mostly by dry-cleaning them. An important event I will never forget was when my wonderful half sister Ethel walked me to a bank and taught me the value of saving money. It's a lesson I've never forgotten.

In those middle years I not only delivered papers but also picked blueberries, strawberries, potatoes, and apples, and shoveled snow. In addition, I was interested in many things, such as magic, stamp collecting, birding, hiking, swimming, skiing, and music. But the passion of my young life was photography.

The early years in school were easy for me. I was either first or second in my class of about sixty until around the eighth grade, or when we started having to do homework. Naturally, my friends were other young scholastic achievers. For example, the boy who also was number one or two was Teddy Stearns, the son of a minister. He and I were selected to be traffic-patrol boys at the early age of eight. I was very proud when I was chosen to carry the American flag at the end-of-year procession when we left our elementary school. My younger sister, Mary, followed another path and was skipping school by the fifth grade.

I was ashamed of the rentals we lived in, and by the time I was in the middle grades I would often leave by the back door and climb a hill so people would not know where my house was. Early on, occasionally I was even ashamed of my father, because he wore working clothes, had a brogue, and sometimes drank beer.

When I was about fourteen and had matured a little, a number of things made me realize I had the finest father in the world. First, he worked harder than anyone I had ever heard of. He would get up about five-thirty in the morning, go to his job with the highway department, come home, and, in summer, mow lawns until eight or nine at night. And they were not ordinary lawns; they were lawns with steep embankments. On weekends he would go to the woods to chop trees and sometimes take me with him to trim branches. He would hire a truck in the fall and bring home trees that were about twelve feet high. On winter nights he would saw them into two- to three-foot lengths to burn. In the winter he worked night and day during every snowstorm, shoveling sand out of the back of a truck onto the icy roads. I tried this once during Christmas break from college and lasted about fifteen minutes. It goes without saying that he was a strong physical specimen.

Somehow our family became acquainted with Mildred Monroe, a wealthy woman in Auburn. My father mowed the lawns at her two houses. When I say our family "became acquainted," it is more accurate to say she became attached to my sister Mary, who was four years younger than I. Visits were scheduled to see her, and she would shower Mary, and to some extent me, with gifts. And when I say she was wealthy, I mean really wealthy. She had a limousine, a chauffeur, and a home in Florida. In the winter we received gifts from her, including fresh fruit, sleds, and skis.

When she was in Auburn my parents would tell us, "Mrs. Monroe would like to see you, so take your sister up the hill." We would then walk up the hill, holding hands as we approached her door. I used to mildly resist because it was Mary who was the attraction. I believe it developed to the point where Mrs. Monroe asked my father if she could adopt Mary. The reply was a strong no. How different her life would have been from the one she lived, and which is actually coming to an end as I write this.

My life went on. There are a number of events I have never forgotten, and all have to do with poverty. Once the Rotary organization invited me to a dinner at the Auburn YMCA. I had a wonderful meal, and they gave me a beautiful ski sweater as a gift. I thought they asked me to attend because I was such a smart

My core family, front row left to right: Mother, Father, my sister Mary; back row: my sister Arlene, me, and my sister Ethel (circa 1945).

student. I later learned that it was because I was poor, and I never again accepted the invitation.

I have mentioned that I became interested in photography. "Interest" is too mild a word. At sixteen I had my own photography business, and desperately wanted a lot of beautiful equipment. In a store, I admired a particular camera. I carefully snuck it out of the store and set a record for pedaling a bicycle across the bridge to Auburn. I never enjoyed or used that camera.

RDO's dad and mom.

As I matured, I came to realize that my father was a selfless, loving, and generous man. He wanted nothing for himself but would do anything for his family. For instance, during the height of my interest in photography, I learned of a photographic enlarger for sale for twenty-five dollars by a private party. That was an enormous amount of money for our family. Somehow my father came up with the money, and I will never forget us walking home at night up a steep hill with that large machine in his arms. I loved it, but should not have let him do it.

Later on, at about age sixteen, I was offered a job selling subscriptions, taking pictures, and selling the proofs and finished portraits for the House of Hinlon photographers, out of Ipswich, Massachusetts. There was one catch: I needed a car. Although he had never owned one himself, my father somehow got me a car. It wasn't much of a car but, again, I shouldn't have had it.

I think the most important thing about my father was his deep love for his family. He idolized his Susie. He couldn't see a single fault in her, and Ethel and Mary weren't far behind. As is traditional with the Irish, his boy was almost the center of his life, but not quite. That position was reserved for Susie.

Years later, when they were getting old, my mother still liked to have her hair done. She would take a taxi to a shop in Haverhill, Massachusetts, and my father would sit in the window at home waiting for her to return.

As for me, I made it through Edward Little High School with marks a little above average. I came through all the experiences of young adulthood basically unscathed. In fact, I had never smoked a cigarette, or had a beer, or known a woman intimately—facts I was not entirely proud of.

❧ 4 ❧

As One with the Sea

The Androscoggin River divides the twin cities of Auburn and Lewiston. There was nothing picturesque about the Androscoggin, with the exception perhaps of the rock falls when the water was high. The problem was that the water didn't stop with being high; it periodically overflowed its banks and flooded large portions of both cities.

Worse, when I was growing up, the water was filthy from human waste, by-products of farm systems, and waste from the mills and shoe shops. For much of the time it gave off an incredible stench. To put it mildly, I didn't like it.

Many years later, a good number of newspaper articles were written about me, including some in the same papers I had once delivered. In one or two of them I made some of these same observations. At an Edward Little High School reunion, Joe Lelansky, a lifelong friend, and several of my classmates asked me if it was really necessary to be so insulting to my hometown.

Anyway, when I was very young, maybe five to eight years old, my parents brought me by train to Old Orchard Beach, a distance of about fifty miles, and I saw the ocean for the first time. This was a seminal event; it overwhelmed me.

It's not that Old Orchard was particularly beautiful, although at one time it was a tony place where Boston's rich and famous went to enjoy the beach. In fact, John Kennedy's parents, Rose and Joseph, met there, and the mayors of Boston customarily spent much of their summers at Old Orchard. Over the years it has become more of a pedestrian carnival town.

It wasn't the atmosphere; it was the ocean itself that touched the very essence of my being. It exhilarated me and filled me with a joie de vivre that would profoundly influence my life.

For most of the latter part of my boyhood I longed to be near the ocean. During evenings filled with the desultory conversations of my family, I'd sneak away to the train station, which was close to where we lived. I would gaze down the tracks and wait for the Boston and Maine Railroad's Flying Yankee train and dream about going to Old Orchard. At that young age I knew with great certainty I wanted to be near, on, or in the ocean for the rest of my life, and that I'd never be satisfied living inland, out of reach of what I so loved. I have in large measure fulfilled that longing.

There were other trips to Old Orchard that I enjoyed. On one outing, when it was cold and gray, I stayed in the water under the pier most of the day. My parents couldn't stop me from shaking most of the night.

I loved everything about the ocean: the ever-changing nature of the sea itself, the magic of the tidal changes, the freshness of the air. After that first exposure, I had little interest in the beautiful ponds and lakes near where I lived and no interest at all in the Androscoggin River.

My half sister Arlene, who had stayed with Guy Holly in Kingfield, eventually moved to Bath, Maine. There she met and married a man named Jimmie Papavacil. He was Greek, and a real Damon Runyan character. Their marriage produced four daughters, my only nieces, and they've always been an important part of my life. Demetra, Joanne, Sandra, and Paula are an integral part of our family.

Some of the joys of those early summers were the surprise visits from Jimmie. Once or twice a season, he would arrive in his old car and announce that we were going to Fisher's Brook, his name for Old Orchard. Both he and Arlene were very generous. We would all stuff ourselves into his car and have a wonderful day, all expenses paid by Jimmie. Arlene's generosity also made it possible for me to spend some weeks at a Boy Scout camp.

5

After High School

I hadn't given much thought to college because I was a lot less than sure whether that was possible as I faced the world in my last year of high school. I had no money, so my goal was to find a place that didn't require any. Thus my early choice was between the Maine Maritime Academy and Northeastern University.

Maine Maritime was a well-known school that, in my junior year, was totally subsidized by the state and federal governments. Many of the boys ahead of me at Edward Little High School whom I considered the most outstanding went there.

Northeastern, in Boston, offered a five-year course with a work-study program that was essentially free. These two institutions met my economic criterion and also my desire to stay in my treasured New England.

In the middle of my senior year in high school, the clear choice was the Maine Maritime Academy, in Castine, the decision based largely on my love of the ocean. Unfortunately, I learned before I graduated that some subsidies had been lost and there would be fees, although they were modest.

I decided to postpone my plans and work a year and then try again. I was warned by many people I respected that I would never be able to do this; I was determined that I could. I began my first year out of high school with a job at Foisey's bakery and a plan to audit a trigonometry course at Edward Little High School.

Foisey's was a small company that made its own food and sold it with a team of twelve employees and about six trucks. It offered baked goods, such as jelly doughnuts, along with sandwiches and terrible coffee. The problem with the coffee was that Mr. Foisey continually added water to it until the trucks went out, claiming it was too strong. My hours were from four in the morning until 11:45 a.m. I then went right to the high school to study the highly stimulating subject of trigonometry from noon to two.

This self-constructed program was mostly successful. In the one year I worked at the bakery I went from the lowest-paid employee (sixty-two cents an hour) to the highest paid (one dollar and sixty cents an hour). The trigonometry audit was less than exciting, but it was okay. I had come to really love the Foisey family, and had some serious thoughts about not leaving. But I did, in August 1951. The Foiseys signed the loan I needed while at Castine.

One of the requirements to be accepted at Maine Maritime was to pass the naval officer physical. This presented a problem, in that no one in my family had teeth. They simply waited until they decayed and then had them extracted. I was well along in this process when I had a clear choice to make. I went to a dentist every morning and afternoon for two weeks to get my teeth fixed. I still have some of those fillings.

6

Off to the Maine Maritime Academy

I got a ride from my home in Auburn to Castine with the parents of a friend who had also been accepted. Maine Maritime produced young officers for the U.S. Merchant Marine and the U.S. Navy and granted a bachelor of science degree, a commission in the Naval Reserve, and a third officer's license in the Merchant Marine.

Graduates were sought after because the institution offered a practical program of academic training and hands-on sea experience. In addition, these young men generally possessed a good work ethic and modest expectations.

I arrived in Castine with mixed emotions. I had real problems with the idea of leaving my well-paying job and entering an institution where I would have to pay to participate in a program that required a good deal of work, both scholarly and physical.

Castine is a quaint coastal town I used to describe as a place where elephants go to die. There were basically no females except for three or four who would never enter the Miss America contest or even the Miss Castine competition, if there was one. This was not exactly an ideal location for a nineteen-year-old Irish lad with raging hormones, and it got worse.

I was assigned to a room with three other guys whose last name also began with the letter O. The room was nicknamed the Shamrock Club, and was called that by everyone. This was not good because it got a lot of attention at a time when the smart idea was to be anonymous. Worse yet, when my past lifestyle became known—that is, no smoking, no drinking, and no ladies—I was looked upon by many, including my roommates, as a weird character, and probably gay. I can assure you I was neither. These qualities listed above would be good for a seminary but not for a school that produced worldly, seagoing ships' officers.

I went to work on this problem. I dropped the Richard and became Dick. I smoked Camel cigarettes during class breaks. I learned to drink beer, and even got to know a lady or two. By the beginning of my second year, you might say I was a leader in all those arenas.

In my plebe year it was discovered that I had been involved in photography. An officer on the staff named Ed Langlois interviewed me and basically gave me one of his collateral duties, that of academy photographer. This was more than fortuitous.

I was suddenly in charge of a photography department of one. I had a Speed Graphic camera and a fully equipped darkroom. This provided me with a safe harbor of refuge, a place to hide from upper-classmen during some of the difficult days of my first year. In later years it was a source of significant income to me.

I photographed every type of group, including sport teams, clubs, and special events. I would post an eight-by-ten photograph on the bulletin board with a sign-up sheet offering copies for one dollar each. The profit margin was incredible—one hundred percent—because I had no costs. I even took most of the graduation formal portraits. I did not know then that I would never be able to create a business model this perfect again.

One very significant thing is that a classmate named Arnold Stinson, known as Rube, befriended me. He was the most popular member of our class. He was about six feet four inches tall, blond, and a great athlete. The fact that we became close friends gave me much credibility and high status. He had one more rather unusual asset: his aunt had given him a brand-new Ford automobile. My hitchhiking days were over. He used to take me home with him for weekends in Cape Porpoise and Kennebunkport. His father, Arnold Stinson, Sr., was a successful lobsterman. One of the features of these getaways was going out lobstering with him on his boat at about four in the morning and coming back five or six hours later.

There was a little gas stove on board and we entertained ourselves on the way in by eating "shorts," the smallest but sweetest lobsters in the world. These are the ones you're supposed to throw back. Rube's father was an accomplished seaman, and he let us know that he thought we were anything but accomplished seamen.

The rest of the weekends were spent on Goose Rocks Beach and exploring the adventures of wonderful Kennebunkport. We had one very exciting weekend that consisted of a drive to Montreal. The purpose of the trip was to see one of Rube's girlfriends, whom he had met on Goose Rocks Beach. Her father was the president of Canadian White Star Shipping Company. I have fond recollections of sitting in a beautiful garden with a butler in full tuxedo serving us beer.

My friend, Midshipman Arnold "Rube" Stinson.

Two weeks later, I was on duty and couldn't leave the academy. Rube loaded his car with five of our other classmates with plans to go to Island Park, a popular dance hall. There was a horrible car crash and all six young men were killed. It was a stunning shock for all of us at the academy. I was a pallbearer for Rube Stinson in Cape Porpoise and for Phil Fox in Braintree, Massachusetts. Rube's girlfriend came to Cape Porpoise for the funeral. I said good-bye to her and never saw her again.

I've been back to Cape Porpoise a number of times, at first alone with his parents and then with my wife, Barbara, who also came to know them. They are both gone now.

Life in Castine was not easy with only two weeks off a year. The academy had—and still has—a training ship called the *State of Maine*, and the student body cruises about three months each year. During my time there, it was to the Caribbean in winter, which was quite an improvement over a Castine winter.

The program was rigorous and physically demanding. I learned a great deal about the seagoing profession, as well as general academic subjects. I became physically stronger and worldly wise.

My senior class photo from Maine Maritime Academy.

The class of 1954 started out with one hundred and two cadet-midshipmen; sixty-two finished the program. Graduates are highly thought of by the shipping industry and the Navy, but they also go on to many other fields. At my graduation, a very proud man from Derryvahalla, Ireland, was in attendance with his family.

Today the academy is much larger and has many more programs, including graduate programs. It's expensive and highly rated academically; it's among the top fifty engineering schools in the country. I've been away a long time, but I know this growth has been accomplished through strong leadership. Two men were in large measure responsible. The first, Ken Curtis, was a senior when I was a freshman. I ended up as his MUG (midshipman under guidance). In this role I did small services for him such as getting him Cokes and snacks during breaks in study hall. Fortunately for me, he was wonderful to me and protected me from some of his wilder classmates. From that beginning we became close friends, and are still friends, as are our wives Barbara and Polly. He was a two-term governor of Maine, served as ambassador to Canada, and was the national president of the Democratic Party. He came back to Castine as president of MMA and had a remarkable record of success there. The second, Leonard Tyler, has been at the academy for some forty years, and just retired as president as this is written. He leaves a legacy of remarkable achievement. He is a thoroughly decent man and produces wonders in an understated way. He and his wife, Bonnie, are pillars of the institution. He is responsible for many of the advanced programs that make the college so admired today.

He has just been relieved as president by William Brennan, who has an interesting background for this position. First, he was born and brought up in Castine. Second, his father served as Commandant of Midshipmen. Brennan served as a high-level executive with The Department of Commerce and NOAA (National Oceanographic and Atmospheric Association).

I have supported the institution for many years with a substantial scholarship fund. I think the interest on the money provides ten or more scholarships; at any rate, that's the number of gracious thank-you letters I receive each year. I also have a grant for the school in my Charitable Remainder Trust.

RDO receiving honorary degree from MMA.

The academy honored me by selecting me as one of the first twelve graduates inducted into its Wall of Fame. I was also a graduation speaker, and received, along with Ken Curtis, an honorary doctorate.

MAINE MARITIME ACADEMY
Castine, Maine 04420
Tel: 207-326-2220
Fax: 207-326-2218

Office of the President   May 17, 1998

CITATION

Richard D. O'Leary, a native of Auburn, Maine, received his first degree from Maine Maritime Academy in the spring of 1954. A Nautical Science graduate, his achievements place him among the outstanding alumni of our college. Throughout his varied and successful career, he has exemplified those characteristics of leadership, dedication, and personal integrity, which we seek to instill in our students.

Upon graduation from Maine Maritime Academy, Mr. O'Leary served as an officer in the United States Navy and as a merchant marine officer aboard freighters bound for Europe and the Far East. He concluded his seagoing career as second officer aboard the legendary superliner, *United States*. Coming ashore in 1962, he accepted a position as Special Assistant to the Superintendent of the United States Maine Maritime Academy. His abilities are duly recognized by that institution with his promotion to Commandant of Midshipmen—the youngest man ever to hold those responsibilities.

Following an executive role with the Maritime Administration in Washington, D.C., Mr. O'Leary provided significant leadership for the development of the Port of Norfolk. His next field of accomplishment was private enterprise, where he created and served as President of C.I. Travel/Cruise International, one of our country's largest travel-shipping companies. By 1990, his fleet of *Spirit*-class ships had grown to fourteen vessels, serving cities on both the Atlantic and Pacific coasts. Today, Mr. O'Leary's operations include travel offices throughout the United States, charter programs for major passenger vessels, and specialized snorkeling expeditions to the Caribbean. His wide-ranging public service activities include a commission as Captain in the Naval Reserve and Vice Chairman of Norfolk Catholic.

In recognition of a distinguished life of achievement and service, we are pleased to bestow the degree of Honorary Doctor of Science on Mr. Richard D. O'Leary.

Walter E. Travis	Leonard H. Tyler
Chairman, Board of Trustees	President, Maine Maritime Academy

I mentioned that I have provided the academy with a scholarship fund and receive about ten to twelve thank-you letters each year. The only guidance I offered was that I would like to see, to the extent possible that preference be given to applicants from the Auburn-Lewiston area of Maine or the Norfolk, Virginia, area. I am very impressed with the way the academy has administered this program, which has been going on for more than twenty-five years. I have chosen to include the first letter, from Brian Gleason, because his letter reminded me of myself. The second letter I just received a few days ago, and I was impressed that Brandon Anthony is from Norfolk, Virginia. I would like to think that this kind of meticulous attention to detail is good for fund-raising. I have also experienced careless inattention, such as from my own high school and some animal shelters.

Brian D. Gleason
Box H-03
Castine, ME 04420
October 4, 2010

Mr. Richard O'Leary
PMB 24
PO Box 413005
Naples, FL, 34101-3005

Dear Mr. O'Leary:

Thank you so much for your generosity in awarding me the Richard O'Leary scholarship. It has helped me immensely in alleviating some of the financial burden that a college education ensues.

This will be my second year at Maine Maritime Academy, and I have absolutely no doubt that enrolling here was the best move I ever made in my life. Growing up in Maine and spending my summers in Friendship, I have always loved the ocean from my first sailboat trip at five months old. As I grew up, I began to dream of working with boats in some capacity on the ocean. I tried several other career focus areas at different schools, but coming to Maine Maritime Academy in 2009 and being accepted into the Small Vessel Operation program honestly felt like I was coming home. It was simply the right place for me to be and now I have a true and clear focus for a successful career in life.

As a non-traditional student of 23 years old, trying to fund my education by myself has not been all that easy. My father's company went under four years ago, leaving me to bear the financial burden of my education alone. I am not afraid of hard work, it is just harder to make the money I make last. I work summers as a boat mechanic and save what I can, but the expense of maintaining a vehicle and paying insurance costs along with living and academic expenses certainly add up. It seems that every year my summer savings erode more quickly than the last, and I find it harder and harder to get by financially.

This scholarship was a much needed leg up and I am very grateful to have received it. In the near future I hope to be the acting captain of a tugboat and a productive member of society. Without your help, this dream may have never been attained. Again I would like to sincerely thank you for generosity.

Sincerely,
Brian Douglass Gleason

————

MMA Box #24
Castine, ME 04420

October 28, 2010
Mr. Richard O'Leary
PMB 24
PO Box 413005
Naples, FL 34101

Dear Mr. O'Leary.

My name is Brandon Anthony and I would like to thank you for the Richard O'Leary Scholarship. I am a senior in the Marine Biology program at Maine Maritime Academy, as well as a member of the Naval Reserve Officer Training Corps where I am currently serving as the Alpha Company Executive Officer. I am also active in the MMA drama club, where I am the head technician and control the lights during performances. I am from Norfolk, Virginia, and I have always been fascinated by the ocean and the variety of organisms living in it. The oceans remain mostly unexplored and the presence of life at the deepest points poorly understood. In addition to my interest in the creatures of the ocean, I have always wanted to be a member of the US Navy. After fulfilling my ROTC obligation, I hope to be able to work for the Navy to study and better understand the undersea world. This scholarship has been and will continue to be beneficial in helping to pay for my room and board here at MMA.

Once again, thank you for your generosity and support.

Sincerely,
Brandon Anthony

PART TWO

❧ 7 ❧

United States
Naval Service

t wasn't long after graduation that I applied for active duty in the Navy. I received my orders, which told me to report to duty on the USS *Wrangell* (AE-12), an ammunition ship berthed in the Brooklyn (New York) Navy Yard.

I was soon aboard a Greyhound bus in my uniform with the one shiny stripe headed for New York. I found my way to the Brooklyn Navy Yard and approached my new home with some trepidation. After climbing the gangway and attempting to salute properly, the officer of the deck ordered the messenger to take Ensign O'Leary's bags to the navigator's room. At first I didn't understand the full impact of what was happening. I thought he meant I was to meet the ship's navigator. When I finally realized that this was going to be my room, I went into a state of shock.

The next day I met Lieutenant Miller, the real navigator, who had moved to another room in preparation for leaving the Navy. Every officer I met on the ship told me that not only was he a crackerjack navigator, but he was also the most respected officer of the twenty officers on board.

The next morning I knocked on the door of the ship's commanding officer, Captain John Corbus, a well-respected submarine squadron commander in World War II. I explained to him that I felt a serious mistake had been made. Although I had studied some navigation and had a little experience with celestial navigation, I had rarely plotted a successful star fix. This meant that, in the case of most of my fixes, the lines of position did not cross in a neat triangle indicating where the ship was. (*Lines of position* are angles measured between a star and the horizon with a sextant and then plotted using trigonometry.)

To my astonishment, Captain Corbus looked at me and said, "Ensign O'Leary, if the Bureau of Naval Personnel says you are qualified, you are qualified." In a very low voice I mumbled something about there being some mistake. I then proceeded to try and convince him that the Bureau of Naval Personnel had indeed made a mistake. To be a good seagoing navigator, you need a good deal of skill and lots of experience. I had neither. I could always tell where we were the first few weeks, though, because we were docked at the Brooklyn Bridge, where two high, colored smokestacks still stand.

The *Wrangell* was a 450-foot Type C2 ship and it was packed with ammunition. Two ammunition ships had blown up in World War II: the *Mount Hood*, in New Guinea, and another one in Halifax Harbor. In each case a crater about one mile in diameter was left at the bottom of the harbor. When this type of ship visits a port, it is customarily assigned to what's called an explosive anchorage three or four miles from any pier. But here we sat in the center of the world's greatest city.

There were some twenty officers on the ship. I was the youngest and the only unmarried one. At first, on my liberty nights, I would go to New York hoping to find a nice girlfriend. This was no small feat. Getting there required walking more than a mile to the gate on Sands Street; boarding a bus to the subway station; then taking a long train ride under the East River to the center of Manhattan, and then more walking. The procedure to return to the ship was reversed, but with a heavy heart, because the hunt for a girl was always unsuccessful.

Most of the married officers lived in New Jersey, and often I took their duty nights so they could go home. There I'd be, cursing my stupidity for sitting on this floating bomb on my off-duty nights.

At about this time I learned the Navy had determined that our crew of 200 did not enjoy high morale. A team of five chief petty officers was dispatched to improve morale by improving the enlisted men's food presentation. I suppose that helped a little, but I could have told them the real problem: most of them wanted to be on a different kind of ship.

The first voyage we made to sea was to Newport, Rhode Island, where we were assigned to the explosive anchorage. Things went fairly well but it was a short trip and I didn't display a lot of confidence. Captain Corbus left for the hospital when we returned to New York; I hope not because of me.

The next voyage was another story. We were ordered to Guantanamo Bay, Cuba, for underway training for several weeks. The trip was an ordeal for me and, I suspect, for a lot of other people as well. The weather was bad, so celestial navigation was out of the question. This left dead reckoning, which entails plotting by way of estimated courses and speeds—not a very accurate method.

Underway training off the island of Cuba was worse. The only navigation was taking bearings with a gyrocompass of the tangents off the island. There were some embarrassing incidents I think I'll just try to forget. I was beginning to think something was wrong. A belief started building in my mind that there was something wrong with the gyrocompass, which is maintained on a Navy ship by the engineering department. I went to see the main propulsion assistant and told him what I thought. I said I'd like to have it checked at the upcoming shipyard overhaul in Philadelphia. He replied in an assertive fashion that there was nothing wrong with the compass but there was something wrong with me. I put in an official work request anyway, and we made it back to New York.

We then left for Philadelphia, and arrived at the mouth of the Delaware River at about dark. The *Sailing Directions* for the Delaware strongly recommended a special pilot be taken aboard to navigate the river because it was full of dangerous turns and confusing lights. Our new, very political captain said no, we would do it on our own—which meant me.

We did pretty well with my recommended courses and he accepted them. At one particularly confusing juncture, he said, "What course do you recommend, Mr. Navigator?"

I said, "I recommend stopping, sir."

We did stop, and aimed a searchlight down to get the markers of the buoys. But the sun came up and we edged our ship into dry dock. Sometime later a remarkable thing happened. The shipyard found that our gyro had sticky bearings, which accounted for a lot of the trouble I had been experiencing.

Things were looking up and so was the girl hunting. In fact, I met my first wife, Marilyn, in friendly Philadelphia.

With Marilyn of Philadelphia aboard the USS Wrangell *in Brooklyn, New York, in 1955.*

We were in the shipyard for about two months, and then prepared to cross the ocean for the Mediterranean and join the Sixth Fleet. Obviously, I had never navigated a ship across an ocean and I was quite anxious. The weather was overcast, which meant there were no stars. In addition, we hit a vicious storm and some 500-pound bombs got loose in one of the holds and were pounding against the bulkhead. We sent some brave boatswain mates down below, who, at great risk, managed to shim the bombs. I worked very hard at my responsibilities, barely sleeping. I was on the bridge almost twenty-four hours a day. A lieutenant from Staten Island, Frank Kelly, suggested that maybe this job was too much for me. I told him I thought he was right.

The sun came out, and so did the stars, and I got some good fixes. On about the tenth day we saw the Rock of Gibraltar and moved into the Mediterranean, and I now had a good gyro for the extensive terrestrial navigation (land points) there.

My experience level was growing and so were my skills and confidence. We received our third captain while in the Sixth Fleet. He was very senior and became the squadron commander, which meant I was navigating a group of about eight ships. They also had to send me their noon positions, so I had some help if I needed it. I didn't.

The squadron comprised service ships, tankers, cargo ships, reefers, and ammunition ships. These ships passed their cargoes to carriers and destroyers while underway. In our case, we took a carrier on the port side and two destroyers on the starboard side and passed bombs and shells on a large steel wire stretched between the ships.

I gained much experience in ship handling, formation steering, and general seamanship. I loved the Navy and had second thoughts about leaving, but I wanted to try what I had been previously trained for—the Maritime Service. I actually stayed two extra months because they didn't have a navigator to replace me.

I was navigating our squadron into Izmir, Turkey, when Lieutenant Frank Kelly, who two and a half years earlier had wondered if this job was too much for me, came to the bridge and said, "I think you are the finest navigator in the whole U.S. Navy."

Experiences like mine, leading a department of twenty men in my first year, are pretty much confined to the military, and they're invaluable, I believe. The Navy really was my first job. My salary was 222 dollars a month, plus 48 dollars for food in the ship's officers' mess.

My father loved that I was a naval officer. He liked that I had good food and looked good in my uniform. He didn't want me to leave. Until my father passed on, I visited with him and my family several times a year. He would plead with me to come down to his job site, usually a sewer, with my uniform on. I hated to but I generally did. Near the end of my Navy tour, I went down with my lieutenant j.g. uniform stripes. We then went to a coffee shop, where he asked the manager, "What do you think of my boy?" When we finished the coffee, he started to pay, and I said to him, "Dad, you will never pay for me again."

In my Navy uniform on first Spirit of Norfolk.

At sea in the Pacific.

8

Maritime Service

I left the Navy in Izmir and started the process of going home. It began with my first air flight, to Naples, Italy. How long you stayed there depended on a second-class Navy seaman whose responsibility was to schedule flights. He received a lot of gifts from officers who wanted to stay longer, in a nice hotel. Everybody did, including me, but for some reason I didn't spring for a gift: too cheap or too timid, I guess.

In any case, the next stop was Port Lyautey, Morocco, for about a week. It was a form of paradise. I did a lot of wonderful things there, including drinking my first martini.

By this point, I knew that my relationship back in Philadelphia with a girl named Marilyn Rubertucci, who called herself Marilyn Roberts, was not going well and I thought that perhaps our romance was over. (From now on, I will refer to her as "Marilyn of Philadelphia.")

The time came to board a flight that was supposed to go to McGuire Air Force Base. It was my first transatlantic flight and, from my perspective, a terrible one. Among other things, we couldn't go to McGuire because of fog. We landed in Dover, Delaware, in what I thought was close to a crash landing. I said I was through with flying. The next day we were offered a flight to Philadelphia to be discharged. I was the only one who took a bus.

I vowed, not very resolutely, not to call or go see Marilyn of Philadelphia. On my first night there, I found myself waiting outside the building in which she worked. I saw a lot of her for the little while before I went back to sea, this time in the Maritime Service.

I also went home to Maine to see my family. My father was very upset and worried that I had given up the wonderful opportunity I had with the Navy.

A week later I once again rode the bus to New York, planning to try to get a job on one of four passenger ships known as the Four Aces, which were owned by American Export Lines. I chose this company because its ships sailed from New York to the Mediterranean, an area I loved. They also sailed on what was known as the sunshine route, a far cry from the North Atlantic.

Before I could get to American Export Lines, however, I made an appointment with the vice president of operations for United States Lines, the largest shipping company in the country. It had fifty freighters and two passenger vessels, the SS *United States* and the SS *America*, both transatlantic liners.

I thought the interview with Captain Tapping went well, and he said I'd be offered a job. Then I made the mistake of asking if any ships were going to the Mediterranean. He was kind of a brusque character and he said, "Do you want a job or don't you? If it's a question of money, we'll advance you the money to join the union." I didn't bother mentioning that this was only my first interview and I that I planned to visit American Export Lines.

Shortly after that, I found myself the third mate on the *American Chief*, of United States Lines, heading out of New York Harbor into the North Atlantic in February. It was good-bye to the sunshine route and the lively Mediterranean.

The *American Chief* was on what was known as the Mersey run (named after Liverpool's Mersey River). The itinerary was New York to Liverpool, Dublin, and Glasgow.

This ship was once again a World War II Type C2. The captain's name was Dunnett, and he was an experienced North Atlantic sailor. He warned me that the run would put the fear of God in me, and it definitely did.

He enjoyed hearing about my Navy service, which was vastly different from what I was about to experience. On a merchant freighter you're alone on the bridge with two seamen who take turns steering and standing lookout. On a Navy bridge you have a cast of thousands. As a navigator, I had someone to hold a stopwatch, someone with a flashlight, someone to record the sextant angle, someone to do counts with a stopwatch to get the precise Greenwich time, and me. The group would run back and forth across the bridge. Captain Dunnett was fascinated that I had actually navigated an ammunition ship up the Delaware River at night. He thought that was lunacy.

The captain was right; the North Atlantic is fearsome in winter. Something happened on that first trip that would foretell my future. While fighting fierce winds and enormous seas, I saw this huge structure with a multitude of lights approach from behind and pass us while it seemed we were almost standing still. I knew what ship it was. It was the greatest ship the world had ever known, the superliner SS *United States*. Our ship could make about ten knots but because it was winter it was probably making seven or eight, and it took ten to twelve days to make a one-way crossing. The SS *United States* was doing about thirty-four knots and made the crossing in four days. I remember wondering what kind of men were on the bridge of that ship.

We continued on to discharge our cargo in three European countries. In Glasgow an incident occurred that concerned me and showed my inexperience. We were loading cases of scotch whiskey. One of my duties in port was to protect the cargo from pilferage. I was given a whistle in case there was any kind of emergency. Trying to look experienced and in control, I was watching the Scottish longshoremen loading the wooden crates of scotch and I happened to notice that one case was tilted on its side and that a good-sized can was attached to it. I also noticed that a longshoreman went over and drank from the can. Of course I immediately blew my whistle. In a matter of minutes the cases were landing harder and there were thirty or forty that were leaking. The chief officer came from out of nowhere and asked what in hell I was trying to do, and didn't I know that it was a hundred-year-old tradition to allow them to have one leaker? I didn't.

Before we left Glasgow, I heard a number of stories about Glasgow longshoremen and scotch whiskey. In those days, Scottish longshoremen actually operated the cranes that lifted the pallets of wooden crates. Sometimes, when the situation got out of hand they would lift some of the longshoremen out of the hold in cargo nets. It was on one of these occasions that they noticed that Big Dan, the watchman, who was sitting in the corner of the ship's hold, had died. As the longshoremen were leaving, one of them said, "What are we going to do about Big Dan?" The near-unanimous reply was "Nothing, leave him there for tomorrow."

We fought our way on the return trip to Boston, enjoying some more of what the North Atlantic has to offer—bad weather. In American ports, no one was allowed to damage the whiskey cases.

Back in New York, I was called to the marine superintendent's office. Miss Downing, who worked in operations, said, "I'm happy to tell you that we're going to put you on the Far East run." I was assigned to a ship called the *Pioneer Main*, a mariner-class ship and, at the time, one of the fastest freight ships in the world. The trips were for three and a half months. I had no idea this might have been part of a plan regarding my future.

I remember sitting on the ship in New York before leaving on the coastwise voyage. This included stops at East Coast ports and then going through the Panama Canal, headed for faraway places I had never seen. For the first time I pondered whether I really wanted to do this for the rest of my life. My pay had increased from about 3,000 dollars a year as a naval officer to more than 12,000 a year, probably twice what the typical college graduate was making. I just wondered if I really wanted to be so far away for so much time. We worked long hours and I wondered if I could have two jobs in New York and do as well.

I had always thought I would be happy to be a ship's captain for the rest of my life. It was at this time that I experienced the first stages of doubt. But it was time to stop thinking and go to sea.

Like most sea voyages, it was an adventure. The Pacific is different. It was 1956 and our planned first port of call was Vietnam. We had the open decks of the 650-foot ship loaded with heavy equipment such as cranes and road machinery, everything lashed down with heavy steel wires about five inches in diameter. We ran into heavy swells and took water over the decks and wrecked all the equipment. We were diverted to Manila, where we offloaded it as junk.

We then completed a round-trip itinerary to Formosa (now Taiwan); Hong Kong; Pusan (now Busan), South Korea; and Yokohama and Kobe, Japan. One of the most favorable impressions for me was Japan. In Baltimore, it had taken us a day to load iron ingots with a huge magnetic crane. I wondered how we would get this offloaded in Yokohama without magnetic cranes. The answer was surprising. First, dozens of neatly packed little meals were brought aboard, contrasting with the ports in the Philippines, Korea, and China, where the longshoremen ate fish heads and rice out of pails with their hands. After that, dozens of heavy gloves that looked like oven mitts wrapped in cellophane were loaded on board.

Then some thirty Japanese longshoremen came aboard, donned the gloves, and threw off those heavy ingots by hand, in about the same amount of time the crane had taken to load them in Baltimore. Next came a crew of female workers, who cleaned the huge, very dirty holds. This was about ten years after the end of World War II, and I came away with a strong impression that the dynamic energy of 90 million people couldn't be permanently subdued.

We sailed the back half of the itinerary and went on to Hawaii for five days before heading for Panama and back to New York. I then had several days off and went to Philadelphia, where I received a phone call from the company asking if

Working cargo in Kobe, Japan, with Owen Clancy, chief officer of Pioneer Main.

I would like to make two relief trips on the SS *United States*. I was flabbergasted, and it's an understatement to say that my answer was yes.

During this period of seagoing travel, I saw my father and the rest of my family just once or twice a year. My father still couldn't write much but he constantly urged my mother to write, which she did poorly. Her main problem, though, was addressing the letters correctly. She would confuse the addresses with the itineraries. For example, while in the Navy the address was simple: Fleet Post Office, New York, N.Y. When in Europe or the Far East, the mail went to United States Lines, N.Y. I would eventually receive some letters months after they had been sent, only after they had done a lot of traveling.

The SS United States *coming into port.*

9

Big U
(SS *United States*)

I knew a great deal about the SS *United States*, or the Big U, as it was affectionately known, as did everyone else involved in maritime affairs. In fact, in those days the general public was very aware of this ship and the ocean liners because of the *Titanic* and, because there were very few airplanes, so the ships were the only practical means of transportation to Europe. The ship was associated with a legendary honor known as the Blue Riband. There was an imaginary 3,000-mile racetrack between Ambrose Light off New York and Bishop Rock off England. For more than a hundred years there was a competition among the world's greatest passenger ships to achieve the fastest crossing.

America, as well as most European countries, produced ships, both sail and steam, to compete. For all those years, from 1850 to 1950, this honor was held by the English, the French, the Germans, the Italians, and the Dutch.

This nautical race was analogous to the later competition to get to the moon. Countries would build ships to display advancements in culture, cuisine, art, technological progress, and, in particular, the speed of the vessels. Ships did not try to compete every year, but rumors would be rampant while they were being built, including much newspaper coverage, much of it inaccurate.

In about 1850, Congress set the goal of winning the honor. The speed record would usually change by small amounts. Victors often won by less than one knot, or one nautical mile per hour. Many of the record holders were household names, such as the *Mauretania*, the *Normandie*, and the *Queen Mary*. America put forth some fine vessels but never won.

Part of the story involves a singular man. He was born August 24, 1886. As a young child he loved drawing pictures of ships, and he read about and studied them as much as he could. He dreamed of building what he called the "Great Ship." He led a rather normal life and attended Columbia University, where he got his law degree, and he actually practiced law for a short time. When he decided he didn't want to practice law, this young man, by the name of William Francis Gibbs, went to J. P. Morgan and asked if he would finance the new naval architecture firm Gibbs and his brother hoped to establish. Gibbs had never taken a course in engineering or in naval architecture. The story goes that Mr. Morgan left the room for a short time, came back, and said yes. Thus the firm of Gibbs Brothers (later renamed Gibbs and Cox) was born.

Gibbs and his brother turned their plans for that Great Ship into their masterpiece, the SS *United States*, and designed every detail. Their firm went on to design about seventy-five percent of all the Navy and Merchant Marine vessels used during World War II.

For fourteen years Cunard's *Queen Mary* held the record for the Blue Riband, with a speed of a little over twenty-nine knots. To reiterate, through the years this honor was often won by less than a knot.

The SS *United States*, on its secret trials off the coast of Virginia, had achieved some remarkable results. She had a full-speed run that reportedly reached more than forty-three knots going ahead and twenty-three knots going astern. A sea trial, of course, is a lot different from crossing the North Atlantic at a sustained high speed. Its true speed, a little over thirty-eight knots, was not revealed until 1977.

By July 3, 1952, the SS *United States* had traveled up from Virginia and was ready to go to sea. She would have 2,000 passengers and a crew of 1,200. Thirteen thousand visitors came to see her off. She carried 123,000 pounds of meat, 60,000 pounds of poultry, and 12,000 gallons of milk. Some grand parties were expected, and she had enough spirits to serve all the bars in New York City—maybe in the entire state.

This brand-new, would-be champion was like none before her. She was fireproof. The only wood on her was the butcher block and the piano; even her bedding was made of fiberglass. She was the first liner to be fully air-conditioned. She had more thrust power built into her propulsion plant than had any other ship ever created. She looked the part, too, with her racy black hull and her rakish red, white, and blue stacks.

Wild rumors floated through the throng that the *Queen Elizabeth* would finally go at full speed and take the record from her sister ship, the *Queen Mary*. It was reported that the Big U would go only gradually up to speed and break the record in future sailings, but despite that, almost everybody believed the *United States* would break every ocean record on her maiden voyage.

William Francis Gibbs, who was on board, had reportedly told the chief engineer not to go above 150,000 horsepower; she had 240,000 horsepower. In the first two days, she averaged an amazing thirty-five knots and then increased to more than thirty-six. She officially won the Blue Riband on July 7, 1952, at 5:16 a.m. Her time was three days, ten hours, and forty minutes; the *Queen Mary*'s fourteen-year record had been beaten by ten hours and two minutes.

Most of the passengers celebrated all night. Margaret Truman, the daughter of the president of the United States, pulled the whistle. Huge conga lines of excited passengers went shaking and snaking through the ship's passageways.

Grand parties were thrown in Le Havre, France, and in Southampton, England. Southampton's welcome was especially joyous even though the Big U had beaten that port's proudest ship. William Francis Gibbs responded to the crowds there: "We honor you for your achievement in ships. We have tried to emulate you."

The *United States* returned to New York and broke the westbound record as well. She flew a forty-foot Blue Riband. She held the record, with no challengers in sight, and she would never relinquish it. The harbor was full of tugboats blowing congratulatory whistle salutes. The streets of Manhattan were mobbed.

She proceeded up the Hudson River to her new home in New York, Pier 86, at about Forty-fifth Street and Twelfth Avenue. Her bow was pointed at the West Side Highway. This is the center of what was known as Steamboat Row, or Luxury Liner Row. Numerous accidents caused by gawkers occurred on the West Side Highway. Crowds gathered at ground level on Twelfth Avenue in the early evenings just to gaze at her.

The entire 1,200-person crew marched in a gala ticker-tape parade, led by the entire regiment of the U.S. Merchant Marine Academy. This was maritime history in full bloom.

My close friend Paul Krinsky, who was the third officer on the record-breaking voyage, had the watch and missed the parade.

Five years later, in 1957, small crowds still gathered at her bow in the early evenings. That September I was standing with my fiancée, Marilyn of Philadelphia,

The SS United States *in 1952 returning to New York after winning the Blue Riband.*

in a crowd of thirty or forty people when she suddenly shouted, "My fiancé is going to become her third officer tomorrow." To my admittedly very mild embarrassment, the crowd cheered and applauded.

The next day I met some seagoing officers whom I had wondered about for a long time. They turned out to be human beings. I was twenty-five and the next youngest was thirty-two.

Most Merchant Marine freight ships have five officers: first, second, and third mates; the chief mate; and the captain. Each mate stood two four-hour watches daily. Each mate had command of the bridge with two able-bodied seamen who took turns steering or standing lookout.

The *United States*, because of her size and speed, had a crew almost double that number. It comprised a third mate and a second mate on each watch with two able-bodied seamen, a navigator, the chief officer, and the executive officer (administrator), along with a Commodore, who was the senior captain in the United States Lines fleet. In this case, the Commodore was John Anderson, an incredible, six-foot seven-inch seaman—a giant of a man in every way.

The third officer on each watch did the navigation, manned the radars, and plotted weather while underway. The second officer supervised and conned (maneuvered) the ship.

The engineering department on a large ship usually consisted of five officers, much like the deck department, which comprised three engineers, a watch officer, and a chief engineer. The engineering department on the *United States*, by contrast, consisted of fifty officers who oversaw two large engine rooms containing two cross-compound turbines delivering 240,000 horsepower, over 100,000 more than any other liner. In addition to the engineering officers, the ship had a large contingent of oilers and wipers and other unlicensed personnel.

The *United States* arrived in New York at eight in the morning and sailed at noon a couple of days later. Summer voyages, of ten days' duration, called on Le Havre and Southampton and then returned to New York. In the winter, when there was less business, we added Bremerhaven, Germany, with passages through the narrow Dover Strait and up the frigid Weser River. This voyage would last for thirteen days.

As I walked to the bridge at eleven in the morning on that sailing day, I was thrilled but tried to show nerves of steel. I'm not sure I succeeded.

Life on the Big U as a deck officer was a difficult one. We worked seven days a week, averaging about seventy hours in a week. There were, however, the rather restful bridge watches during the four-day crossings. (Most ships take ten days to cross, and even the biggest and fastest new cruise ships need six. And they do this only in summer, when the weather is best.)

When putting into ports, the officers manned the bridge and supervised line handling and tugs and the loading and offloading of mail, silver ingots, about a hundred cars, and oh, yes, the passengers. The ship was scheduled to meet boat trains in Le Havre and Southampton that would carry passengers to Paris and London.

After I was on the ship a year or two, my mother and father came to see Marilyn and me in Bergenfield, New Jersey. I decided to take them to visit the ship. It turned out to be a bit of an adventure.

My father was very excited. I thought my mother was, too, but she wasn't so easy to read. The first notable thing was that she was afraid to use the escalator to get to the upper level of the pier. It took some ingenuity on my part to find a freight elevator in which she could ride. I gave them a tour of the ship, and we ended up on the bridge and in the chartroom. I explained to them, in a very painstaking way, what transpired there and what I did. At the conclusion my mother said, "This is very nice, Richard, but what do you do for work?"

My father was an important part of my life during these years. To put it mildly, he worried about me constantly. He insisted that I go to the pier and call him as soon as the ship docked. I explained that when we docked I had certain duties to perform. He never accepted this; he felt there was no excuse not to call by eight-thirty. We more or less compromised on about nine a.m.

The calls concerned discussions about how much he worried about me. He also reminded me many times of the Seventh Commandment, "Honor thy Father and thy Mother," which I thought I did but I tried to do better.

He followed everything he could read or listen to about ships. One day he was talking about a particularly bad gale he had heard about. I assured him that I was on the best and safest ship in the world. "But you're on the North Atlantic Ocean," he said. As he got older, I reciprocated his worries. I would visit him in Haverhill, Massachusetts, where he was living. When it was time to go, I'd always leave the car and go back, and he would invariably come down to the first floor. My purpose was to look, for what I thought might be the last time, into his blue eyes. I would then be depressed for an hour or so as I drove away. This went on for years because he was a gentle but exceedingly strong man, and he lived for many more years.

There really was no social life for officers on the Big U. Other than the good food in the small private dining room, there were almost no pleasurable things to do. We had a small lounge in the middle of our ten staterooms, but it seemed like every fan on the ship was piped into it and none of us ever went in. We weren't permitted to socialize with passengers or enter their lounges. It didn't matter that much because we were so busy. After I was there for about three years,

RDO with binoculars.

we were allowed to go to the first-class movies. This seemed a juvenile privilege for men who carried a heavy load of responsibility.

Adding to the difficulty for those who lived full-time on board were the time changes. The total time change was five or six hours, depending on daylight saving time. All the ship's clocks were advanced six hours going east to France and turned back six hours coming back; each night all the clocks were electrically advanced or turned back an hour and a half. This meant, for those of us making round-trips, that the hours of meals and sleeping changed by six hours each way. For those of us on the bridge, there was no difference between night and day.

I was ostensibly assigned to the Big U for two trips to relieve a permanent officer. I guess I did okay because the senior officers communicated to the company about me. Although I knew the name of the person I was replacing, I never met or heard of him again, and I became a permanent officer. I stayed for five years and made more than 240 crossings. The pay was very good.

A lot of things happened during those years. For one, I married Marilyn of Philadelphia and we had three beautiful daughters, Lauren, Leslie, and Megan.

In my spare time aboard ship, of which there was little, I kept a darkroom in my room, and I finished a photo essay called "Sailing Day." I also completed a very difficult two-year course called Modern Business, which was primarily correspondence and assignments, through the Alexander Hamilton Institute.

I met many celebrities, as the commodore would bring them to the bridge and leave them there before they rejoined him in his suite for refreshments and cocktails.

One of the most important aspects of my job on the ship was that I was usually on the bridge during docking and undocking. I had the privilege and great learning experience of observing as some of the greatest seamen in the history of the world handled the ship. I include Commodore John Anderson himself, Richard Ridington, our chief officer, and a Southampton docking pilot named Bertie Strowger. I watched them and learned a great deal, mainly coolness and the ability to become part of the ship itself.

National advertisement for Eastman Kodak with RDO and a Girl Scout.

Deck officers were required to become members of the Masters, Mates, and Pilots Union, which we all had very little interest in. I was doing quite well and was about to relieve a second officer for one trip to provide him some vacation time. An officer, whose name I won't mention, was assigned by the company to take my place as third officer. When he came aboard, he complained to the union that he had been with the company longer than I had. The Coast Guard had to come back and sign him on as second officer for the trip and put me back to third. This slowed my progress, but only for a while.

Another incident involving the same union happened when I was going on vacation. The union was on strike and, although I was on vacation, they called me and told me I had to picket in Jersey City at eight in the morning. A very unhappy Richard O'Leary arrived at seven-thirty, just as 200 longshoremen were coming to work a large cargo ship. I took the picket sign from my predecessor, who had had a quiet night. Longshoremen came up to me saying things like, "Why don't you go have a cup of coffee so the boys can go to work?" I made it clear that I didn't want to deprive them of work and that I would call the union. I called them in Manhattan and told them I had no interest in this.

THE S.S. UNITED STATES
A Glimpse of a Bygone Era
excerpted from *Port Folio Magazine*

*Brochure detail from C.I. with RDO and
actress Jane Wyman.*

The union told me not to leave under any circumstance and that they would send more men immediately. It was a tense forty-five minutes, with threats and a little shoving, before anyone else came, but I didn't leave even though I really wanted to. When a car carrying a top union vice president and four new picketers finally showed up, I was praised and told I could go home. I felt like anything but a hero but was happy to go on vacation.

About a month later, someone on the Big U bought me a copy of the union newsletter. It had a long story about my supposed heroism, and I was urged to run for union vice president. I later had an opportunity to appoint the vice president, who later became president of the union, to a college advisory board that I controlled.

Bob Dickinson, the former president of Carnival Cruise Lines and a close friend of mine, insisted I include the following dog story. The main characters, including the dog, are no longer with us. Some of this may not be entirely accurate and it might be a little exaggerated in some respects, but the incident did happen.

The commodore's dog was named Chodopeg, and his tiger, or personal butler, was named Pete. The Big U had an animal kennel that was used to board various pets during the voyage. It even had a fire hydrant on deck for urination purposes. The attendant's name was Paul.

For one voyage, the commodore was on vacation, and the staff captain was relieving him. The staff captain had a more excitable personality than the commodore.

One morning Pete found Chodopeg dead, and notified the staff captain, who had been asleep in his own stateroom.

Upon learning the news, he went into panic mode: "Oh my God," he said, "the commodore's going to kill me, the commodore's going to kill me!"

He convened a preliminary meeting of the principal officers and opened with, "The commodore's going to kill me!"

Plans were made for a funeral that very day, including the construction of a small casket that would be released overboard with appropriate ceremony and a flag.

At a second meeting four hours later, the officers met again. After checking all the details, such as stopping the ship and entering the latitude and longitude in the logbook, the staff captain was satisfied. He sent for Pete, the steward, and asked, "Where's the body?"

Pete answered, "Paul has taken care of Chodopeg."

"What do you mean, 'Paul has taken care of Chodopeg'?" exclaimed the staff captain.

"Paul threw him overboard," replied Pete.

"Threw him overboard?" shouted the staff captain. "The commodore's really going to kill me!"

The ship did stop, the funeral took place, the entry was made in the logbook, and the casket was lowered overboard with appropriate photographs of the ceremony. The commodore didn't kill the staff captain, although I'm not sure he ever learned all the details. The pictures exist to this day.

Sailing the North Atlantic was a rigorous way of life and provided many kinds of experiences. It was the weather, though, that made it so difficult.

There isn't much good weather at all. In the spring and fall, most of the time it was gray or foggy. On many westbound trips to America we left France and saw nothing but fog from the pier in Le Havre to the dock in New York.

As with anything, of course, you get used to it. Traveling at that speed with no visibility is a frightening prospect, but when you do it many times over many years, you can get blasé.

Usually it was a nonevent, but once in a while, particularly when traveling over the waters where the *Titanic* went down, I would get spooked. Then for some time I couldn't take my head out of the radar.

The distance across the Atlantic is shorter the farther north you sail because of the great circle effect, which is due to the curvature of the earth. We received reports of where the most-southern icebergs were spotted by plane. We were required to sail a safe distance south of them. In fact, I've never seen an iceberg other than while on a pleasure cruise in Alaska.

In winter the seas were very rough, sometimes unbelievably rough. We were always trying to go as far north as we could because of the great circle effect, so we were in some fairly high latitudes when the weather was at its worst.

North Atlantic gales, which persist most of the winter months, are terrible. A tropical storm, even a hurricane, is relatively small, maybe a couple of hundred miles in diameter, so the fetch is a relatively short distance. (*Fetch* is the unobstructed distance over which the wind blows across the surface of the water, enabling seas to build to huge heights.) A true North Atlantic gale can be 800 to 1,000 miles in diameter, creating an enormous fetch and great seas.

The *United States* could handle seas very well, and sustained damage just once in all the time I was aboard. It happened in the worst weather Commodore Anderson had ever seen. We were hove-to for more than a day with mountainous seas. We were taking whitewater over the bow, which was seventy feet in the air. Spray from heavy seas broke off a range light more than a hundred feet in the air. When we disembarked the passengers in England and in France, I think most of them had probably lost their interest in North Atlantic seagoing. In fact, I'm convinced that God didn't intend for people to be out on the North Atlantic in winter.

The ship was divided into three classes: first class, cabin class, and tourist class. Each had its own galley, dining room, movie theater, and lounge. The classes were divided with gates and fiberglass locking devices, which could be broken with a shove in case of emergency. We had someone replacing them almost full-time because passengers would break them to go adventuring. There were three Meyer Davis orchestras on board. The food, although it varied some by class, was superb. The ship, with all her speed, was an experience everyone should have at least once.

Officers lived quite an austere life. The bridge officers ate in a small private dining room, usually only two or three at a time because of bridge responsibilities. When I first saw our menu, I thought I'd never get tired of the food. For instance, we often had ten kinds of soup to choose from. I still love soup. But much to my surprise, I found myself eating the same very simple things trip after trip, and I did get tired of the food.

In early 1962 a young Maritime Administration trainee was sent aboard to be an observer of ship operations. Part of the plan was to have him on the bridge for several watches. None of my esteemed colleagues wanted him on the bridge with them, so I said I would take him with me. He was an agreeable young man and I liked him. In our conversations I mentioned I had finished the Alexander Hamilton Institute course in business. He asked me why I would choose to do all

RDO's official Coast Guard discharge from his last voyage on the SS United States.

that work, and I told him I thought it might come in handy, especially if someday I wanted to go ashore.

He then told me about a job at the U.S. Merchant Marine Academy. It was as the assistant to the superintendent, Vice Admiral Gordon McLintock, and he asked if I would like him to submit my name. After thinking about it, I told him to go ahead. Some of the officers on the Big U were graduates of Kings Point. They told me that he would never hire me, mostly because I was from Maine and he had a social pool of friends to choose from.

The young man also mentioned that McLintock was a perfectionist, a politician, and regarded by some as brilliant but difficult. I learned he had been searching for an assistant for close to three years, and had interviewed more than 200 people for the job. This all seemed incredible to me, and a little worrisome.

On a snowy day I drove from New Jersey to Kings Point, which is in Great Neck, New York, with Marilyn of Philadelphia, and saw the very beautiful U.S. Merchant Marine Academy for the first time. It was built on the former summer estate of Walter Chrysler. The administration building is the former Chrysler residence and is reminiscent of the White House. It is on what was formerly known as the Gold Coast, overlooking Long Island Sound with the buildings of Manhattan in the distance.

I entered the building and then the vice admiral's office, and saw for the first time the man who would become my mentor and change my life. I thought

RDO lamenting the demise of the SS United States.

the interview went well; the most and only telling thing he said was "You'll never get rich working for the government."

Marilyn of Philadelphia and I left and drove into New York City. We went to P. J. Clarke's, the famous East Side bar. "The Poor People of Paris" was playing on the jukebox. I told Marilyn of Philadelphia that if he didn't hire me, he was a crazy man, and I wouldn't want to work for a crazy man. I was twenty-nine years old.

I didn't hear anything for a month, and then I received a call and learned I had the position. It was expected that creating the position would get through the red tape of government regulations in a couple of months, but it took more than four.

After I let it be known that I was accepting the position, two company vice presidents talked to me about my glorious future with United States Lines, but despite the new job's almost fifty percent pay cut, my mind was made up.

The same officers who had admonished me earlier now asked, "Why do you think he chose you?" I replied, "I guess he wanted the youngest officer on the SS *United States.*"

The *United States* has for years been laid up in various places in deplorable condition. I learned recently that she has been purchased by a conservancy with some hope of restoring her and taking her to a major city to serve as a tourist attraction. I'm glad.

SS United States *at sea.*

The administration building at Kings Point, the former Chrysler residence.

RDO, a midshipman, and the academy mascot.

RDO and Vice Admiral McLintock.

❧ 10 ❧

The U.S.
Merchant Marine
Academy
Kings Point, New York

ice Admiral McLintock had an interesting background. He was born in Scotland into a seagoing family. One grandfather owned a fleet of sailing vessels and the other owned one of the world's largest shipyards.

In 1930 he was appointed a steamship inspector by the Department of Commerce. Before World War II he supervised the licensing of Merchant Marine officers. During the war he was chief inspection officer for the War Shipping Administration and the United States Maritime Commission. In 1948 he became the fourth superintendent of the U.S. Merchant Marine Academy.

On one beautiful August morning, I presented myself in all my splendor with a new uniform and more stripes at the U.S. Merchant Marine Academy. The admiral was not there. He had gone to the opening of the second level of the George Washington Bridge. I learned that he was a bit of a celebrity and attended many of New York City's poshest parties and social events.

I saw him for the first time after the initial interview late that afternoon. It was then that he told me of his plans for my indoctrination into this prestigious academy.

He had a beautiful office that had been Mr. Chrysler Sr.'s bedroom, with ramps to prove it. Mr. Chrysler was crippled during part of his life; at least we thought he was.

There was a room between his office and one that housed two secretaries. That room had been Mr. Chrysler's library, I think, and had been empty for two or three years.

The admiral explained his plan to move a desk from that office into his. The desk would be placed next to his so that all correspondence and phone calls would go first to him and then to me.

After a month, the desks would be reversed and all correspondence and phone calls would go first to me and then to him. It turned out to be a wonderful experience. The admiral was a wonderful raconteur with hundreds of stories to tell and a great sense of humor. At the end of two months he said, "Let's do it for one more month." I've never laughed more in any other three-month period in my life.

Many times, especially early on, important visitors came to see him: academics, politicians, and other bigwigs. Most expected me to leave when they were there, but he told me never to go, and to the embarrassment of some, I never did.

Soon after I arrived, I received a jolt. I asked the then assistant superintendent when the uniform changed from khakis to blues. He said in about six weeks, but that I probably wouldn't have to worry about that. He explained that the alumni association was working on getting me fired, and perhaps McLintock would be fired as well. It was nothing personal, he said, but it was that the association thought it was wrong that the admiral couldn't find one assistant out of the hundreds of Kings Pointers who had graduated each year. This was more than unsettling because I had just resigned from one of the most prestigious and highest-paid jobs in the seagoing world.

The alumni kept their word and tried hard, but they didn't succeed. At the end of the three months the admiral said to me, "You go run this institution." I moved into the beautiful office next to his, but I did not, or even attempt to, run the institution.

Somehow at that young age I was quite conservative, and I'm going to try to write this particular section with a certain amount of delicacy.

It turned out to be a wonderful working relationship for everyone. I think I was wise enough to use my obvious influence judiciously. I remember going to the Officers' Club on Friday evenings and being engulfed by petitioners for jobs, raises, furniture, projects, and myriad other desires. I loved it, and felt singular,

The Merchant Marine Academy at Kings Point, half-time show conceived by RDO.

but I always realized this was transferred power and I tried to make it clear that I understood that.

A short visit to the beautiful grounds of Kings Point would convince anyone that it is serene and peaceful. That's true, to some degree, but any college with a thousand intelligent students and all the intrigues of academe makes for a very lively place.

Those who attend the academy are of high academic caliber. They have to be in the top ten percent of their high school class, with high college entrance scores, and be nominated by a member of Congress or a senator. Some came because it was free, or because they didn't get accepted at another academy, or because others—for example, their parents—influenced them.

The academy was established in 1943 with a rather rigid program modeled after that of the Naval Academy. The subtle goal of many of these young students was to turn it more toward a liberal arts program, which created certain tensions. When I arrived, many of the officers and faculty were older—from the Second

World War era—and resistant to change. Not all, but some of the many day-to-day problems were a result of these pressures.

Another problem at that time was in the area of disciplinary regulations and procedures. The academy, like the others affiliated with the federal government, operated under honor and demerit systems, which involved a good deal of administrative record keeping. There was also a book of procedures for serious offenses, which were called first-class offenses. The book outlined the duties of various faculty boards to conduct hearings and recommend punishments, including dismissal. There were a number of appeal procedures, among them a final review by the superintendent.

Dismissal could also occur through an aptitude hearing before a faculty board after a student had exceeded the maximum number of demerits. Again, there were a number of appeal and review procedures, these too culminating in a review by the superintendent.

In the case of a recommendation for dismissal, it was forwarded to the Maritime Administration in Washington, D.C., for final approval. In every case during my first years at the academy, political interest would develop because the student and family and friends would contact members of Congress. The cases would be returned with instructions to "punish short of dismissal." This had a terrible effect on the institution and on the student body.

Admiral McLintock, who headed the school for twenty-two years, was happy to leave the running of the regiment of midshipmen largely to others. He involved himself in some very important projects and attained some remarkable successes.

Instead of flaunting my obvious influence, I chose to do the opposite and tried to be helpful to everybody. People soon learned that I wanted to be a positive influence in all the issues that came before me. They learned that in order to get things done, it was best to enlist my help.

From private sources, Admiral McLintock raised the money to build a magnificent interdenominational chapel. Its main feature was a listing of every person killed in the Merchant Marine in the two world wars. Each name was inscribed by a calligrapher on vellum in a glass case modeled after the one at St. Paul's Cathedral in London. This was all accomplished without any government money, and it was a remarkable piece of work.

He was the one who, in the early years, fought to accredit the school so students could obtain four-year degrees, and he oversaw its reaccreditation during the six years I was there. He also implemented the construction of a beautiful library. Beyond these achievements, there was no stronger advocate of the proposition that the academy existed to produce seagoing officers for the Merchant Marine and the Navy.

It was during this period that President John F. Kennedy was assassinated. Obviously this was a traumatic event for the whole country, and it was especially so for me. I revered him, and made a private vow to myself that I would try to enter politics.

The academy was a wonderful laboratory for developing some of the skills that would be helpful to that end. I had a whole student body to practice my speaking and writing skills on, and, more important, to help me develop my judgment in leading people.

I held the notion of trying to enter the political field for a long time, but years later, in Virginia, after I had founded and developed my company somewhat, a group of Republican state leaders led by Federal Judge Robert Doumar came to my office. They offered me the nomination for the Virginia State Senate and I declined. I jokingly told people it was because I had accumulated about 500 dollars in my bank account.

It was actually because my zeal for the profession had lessened as I matured and became more aware of the demands and workings of the political world. Another reason, perhaps even more compelling, was that I had experienced a taste of capitalism and loved the prospect of creating economic activity where none had existed.

At the academy, I was generally involved in every major problem or program that developed. Then, about halfway through my six years there, an event occurred that changed my focus.

Justice William Douglas of the Supreme Court was visiting the admiral for dinner. The midshipmen staged a hunger strike in the mess hall, claiming the food was terrible, and a paper of grievances was produced. The New York newspapers picked up the story, and the Department of Commerce launched an investigation. At that time, a group of officers headed by a regimental officer was in charge of the midshipmen. The school was in crisis mode and the officer in charge, an older and experienced

Our long-time friends, Federal Judge Robert Doumar and his wife Dot.

man, was relieved. Admiral McLintock named me to the position. It was not a good situation to step into.

I was well known by all the officials in the Maritime Administration in Washington, who had ultimate control over the academy. Before I formally accepted the responsibility, I reached an understanding with the Department of Commerce officials. I said I intended to be fair to these young students, but I expected to be backed up when a dismissal was necessary.

The investigation was led by a man named George Gould. I told him that if he wanted these midshipmen to lie, cheat, and steal, he didn't need me. He was wholly supportive of me and I accepted the responsibility. He ultimately did wonderful things for the school.

These were difficult times for a while, but I was granted full freedom of action. I began with new approaches and was helped by being much closer in age to the students than my predecessor had been.

There were some major administrative changes as well. All the departments were put directly under my management: the regiment, food service, ship's stores, athletics, waterfront, and public works. The only exceptions were the faculty and the academic dean. The position was eventually called Commandant of Midshipmen, as at the other academies.

I held many listening sessions with the student leaders and treated them like adults. Mostly I solicited their ideas about how to improve the academy, and they had many, a good number of which were quite responsible.

We built new wardrooms for the seniors with money I raised, and the students did the work themselves. We created programs to increase the physical fitness of the regiment. We built a rather ingenious merit program to go with the demerit system. We created special events, such as Kings Point Weekend, for which students designed all the happenings. Marching in formal reviews had always been a sore point, but right in the middle of that weekend they planned a formal review in order to impress their girlfriends.

At first, disciplinary problems continued, a few ending in dismissal. One became an important legal case. It was an aptitude case; a young man named Wasson had exceeded the maximum number of demerits. His final offense was that he led a number of other students in an abortive attempt to throw the regimental commander (the student leader) into Long Island Sound. Before the case had gone through all the academy's procedures and hearings, it was challenged by the American Civil Liberties Union. Attorneys there asserted that academy regulations did not afford due process to students. They contended that a full adversarial proceeding with legal representation was necessary.

The case reached the Second Court of Appeals in New York, at that time the second-highest court in the land. I was the principal figure for the defense and was represented by three Department of Justice attorneys.

The case went on for weeks; the academy prevailed on all counts. The court based its verdict on some statements from Associate Supreme Court Justice Felix Frankfurter. The verdict said that an adversarial trial was not necessary in a scholastic environment as long as the institution's own rules were meticulously followed and fundamental principles of fairness were achieved. This was in 1968, and it was then the landmark decision in the United States regarding academic due process. I actually tried to help Mr. Wasson after his dismissal.

The following is a letter asked for and obtained during a discussion of the Wasson case between the editor in chief of *Hear This*, the student newspaper, and Captain R. D. O'Leary. Captain O'Leary had just received this letter prior to this discussion and, thinking it a fitting epilogue to the Wasson case, I therefore asked permission to print it.

Friday, June 7, 1968

Dear Captain O'Leary,

I am sorry that I wasn't able to come to graduation but I was in the middle of license examination. I took the examination here in Corpus Christi as the Baltimore inspectors were snowed under with people from the MEBA school and wouldn't have been able to get to me until the first of July. I finished the entire examination in only 15 1/2 hours and had a 91.6 average. I think that I am pretty fortunate when one considers how bad things could have been under the circumstances. I feel that I owe most of it to you and wish that there were some way that I could express my appreciation and extreme gratitude, however I cannot think of any way to do it properly. My only regret is that, according to the inspector, I will need some 700 days of sea time before the license will become permanent. I had hoped to be a second mate in two years but now I guess that it will take a good deal longer. I wish you all the luck possible in your new job and cannot help but think that you will do well.

Very truly yours,
s/Robert Wasson

I loved life at the academy and much of the improvement I was able to bring about was because I had the full support of the admiral. I've been fortunate to enjoy many successes, but when people ask me what my favorite period was, I usually answer that I think it was this one, working closely with students. In the school paper's editorials it was dubbed "The Era of Good Feelings." It wasn't because I made life easier for them; on the contrary, it was probably because I engaged them in the management of the school. That worked miracles.

We had so many successes. You could feel it in the air. We developed many programs and approaches. They were innovative and smart, and most came from the student body. The institution was suddenly full of spirit and pride.

These were busy times. I worked long hours, including Saturday events; traveled with the admiral; and went to Naval Reserve meetings one night a week. I

Top: RDO and daughters at King's Point about 1964. Bottom: RDO and daughters in Maine years later.

took some courses at New York University and then entered the graduate business program at Adelphi University, the oldest university on Long Island. I was awarded a fifty-percent graduate-tuition scholarship and attended at night. With the required A-minus average, I earned a master's degree in business administration.

Those six years at Kings Point were a heady time, and they were among the best of my life. Admiral McLintock gave me innumerable opportunities and I'll never forget them or the young men I had the privilege of working with. I knew, however, that it was time to move on, although I didn't know where I wanted to go.

Those years there were also wonderful ones for my family. We lived in a big beautiful house. Admiral and Mrs. McLintock were lovely to our daughters. Megan was born early in our residency there, and I took her from the hospital to the McLintocks' house, even before bringing her home. The McLintocks, who had no children of their own, always had special Thanksgiving and Christmas dinners for our family on a day near the holidays so they wouldn't interfere with our personal celebrations.

The three girls, especially Lauren and Leslie, the older two, loved campus life. They were well known by the midshipmen and had picked out their favorites among them. They would go to the academy movies and try to sit behind those favorites. When things were stressful with the regiment, I'd often receive humorous notes threatening to kidnap them and hold them hostage until some decision of mine was reversed. It was all great fun and the girls still remember it happily.

The work was satisfying, and I retain countless memories of my happy years there. I'll describe one rather simple event and illustrate it with a picture.

During football season, the students asked if they could have what they called an Optional Hats Day. This meant that as they marched into the mess hall to the drumbeat, they could wear any kind of hat they wanted. They certainly came up with some imaginative creations. After I gave the green light to the day, I remembered a tricornered hat the admiral had received in New York City at the world premiere of the film *Mutiny on the Bounty*.

I went to his office and asked if he still had the hat. He did. I asked him to trust me and meet me in the galley behind the dining room. I ran to his house, found the hat, and took it to the galley. I asked him to come out wearing it when I called him. I went to the microphone and told the room something unfortunate had happened and that it was my fault. I said the superintendent was upset about the hats and had come to talk to them about it. He walked in with the tricornered hat. The picture speaks for itself. You must understand that the admiral was considered a rather pompous personality, which he certainly was not.

Admiral McLintock wearing his tricornered hat.

Another memory is of the academy in summer when my parents were visiting. Admiral McLintock walked over to my backyard, something he never did. There he was, in all his dignity, and my father said, "What do you think of my boy?"

I have on a couple of occasions mentioned Paul Krinsky. Paul, a graduate of the academy, had established the highest academic record at the time of his graduation. He was chosen to be the third officer on the maiden voyage of the SS *United States*. When I arrived five years later on that same ship, my fellow officers spoke glowingly of him. He had returned to Kings Point and was teaching navigation in the Naval Science Department.

When I came to work at the academy, I was somewhat in awe of him. I didn't see him for a while so I sought him out, and we developed a friendship. In fact, I played some role in getting him out of the faculty and appointed dean of admissions. After I left the academy, he demonstrated that he didn't need any help from me; he went on to become the academic dean and the superintendent.

We became close friends. Years later, we often stopped at Kings Point with our private yachts on the way north to Maine. Paul's wife, Audrey, cooked for us, arranged for us to do laundry, baked cookies, and did other wonderful things not normally associated with the lofty position of wife of the superintendent. There is a garden at Kings Point named after her. The Krinsky family journeyed to Norfolk for our daughters' weddings. Their grand piano is in our living room in Maine, a gift from them when they left the academy.

As I write this, I'm reminded of a laugh-out-loud incident that occurred when they were visiting us in Hyannisport, Massachusetts. We were headed to the beach with their two sons, David and Ross. Paul didn't have his bathing suit and his younger son, Ross, asked, "Why not?" Paul answered that he didn't feel like getting wet.

Playing in the water, Ross was close to a tidal current and Paul admonished him about the danger. A little bit later Ross was actually being carried away from shore by that current. Paul dove in fully clothed. On the way home, in soaking-wet clothes, Paul was muttering about how Ross would not learn from the

With Paul Krinsky at Kings Point.

experience when Ross muttered back, "Dad, I thought you said you didn't want to go swimming."

When I retired, Paul flew to Norfolk and also wrote a wonderful letter for my memory book that I treasure.

When I left the academy, I accepted a position as director of cargo promotion within the Maritime Administration. The government paid for our move to Washington. I realized within a couple of weeks that this work was not for me. I lasted a few months and knew I would have to leave even if I had to pay back the relocation money.

While I was there, I was nominated for the Arthur Fleming Award for outstanding work at Kings Point. The administration didn't want me to leave and offered me a position as maritime attaché for the embassy of Rio de Janeiro, London, or Rome, but Marilyn of Philadelphia said all of those cities were too far from her mother and Philadelphia. I was not required to reimburse the moving money.

At about the same time, a group of three gentlemen representing the Norfolk Port and Industrial Authority invited me to lunch. They explained the details of the position of deputy general manager. I listened carefully, then explained that I was a Northerner and doubted if I would be happy in the South. The one person who had hardly spoken was a man named J. J. Gara, who it turned out was chairman of the board. Suddenly he said, "Goddamn it, you don't look entirely stupid, so why don't you come down and see what we have to offer?" So I did.

Government work in Washington was not for me. We lived in Alexandria and I started commuting to the GAO building on Fifth and G streets. First I took the bus, and in the summer, at the end of each day every piece of clothing had to

Farewell to Kings Point.

be dry cleaned or washed. Then I changed to a carpool and that was not good. There were six of us, and the other five were experts on the routes and back streets around Route 95. They knew exactly what lane they should be in at what moment and where and when to divert to alternative routes. Every sixth week, when I drove, was a disaster. I never made a correct move and they were thoroughly exasperated with me.

Earlier I mentioned work—almost nobody did any. I was disgusted with well-paid executives dressed up, coats on, waiting for the tick of the clock that would set them free to begin the exodus home.

I've never felt so strongly that nobody cared if anybody did anything. I was supposed to be working on finding more cargoes for American ships. It seemed that nobody wanted any. I did, in the few months I was there, develop a landbridge concept. It involved moving fruits and vegetables across the country in refrigerated unit trains and then onto American ships primarily from Norfolk. I made one major presentation; it was well received but eventually ignored, so I took it with me. This, in fact, was what interested the Norfolk Port Authority in me.

After that, when I was in Washington with friends walking past the Hart Senate Office Building, they would point out that a lot of people seemed to be working late, as all the lights were on. I told them I thought this was the nature of the problem: there should be a renewed effort to get people home on time without doing any more harm. The poem "Exiled," by Edna St. Vincent Millay, captures how I felt during this period.

Exiled

Edna St. Vincent Millay

Searching my heart for its true sorrow,
This is the thing I find to be:
That I am weary of words and people,
Sick of the city, wanting the sea;

Wanting the sticky, salty sweetness
Of the strong wind and shattered spray;
Wanting the loud sound and the soft sound
Of the big surf that breaks all day.

Always before about my dooryard,
Marking the reach of the winter sea,
Rooted in sand and dragging drift-wood,
Straggled the purple wild sweet-pea;

Always I climbed the wave at morning,
Shook the sand from my shoes at night,
That now am caught beneath great buildings,
Stricken with noise, confused with light.

If I could hear the green piles groaning
Under the windy wooden piers,
See once again the bobbing barrels,
And the black sticks that fence the weirs,

If I could see the weedy mussels
Crusting the wrecked and rotting hulls,
Hear once again the hungry crying
Overhead, of the wheeling gulls,

Feel once again the shanty straining
Under the turning of the tide,
Fear once again the rising freshet,
Dread the bell in the fog outside,—

I should be happy, —that was happy
All day long on the coast of Maine!
I have a need to hold and handle
Shells and anchors and ships again!

I should be happy, that am happy
Never at all since I came here.
I am too long away from water.
I have a need of water near.

I would like to end this section with something I suppose is unusual. Vice Admiral McLintock and I more or less lost touch with each other for a while— but not for long. We found each other again and had many more wonderful times, including when Muriel McLintock christened one of our *Spirit* ships. At his request, I was honored to do his eulogy both at the McLintock Chapel at the Merchant Marine Academy and at Arlington National Cemetery. I think it appropriate that I close this chapter with that eulogy.

Admiral McLintock on the balcony of our new CI building on the Norfolk waterfront.

Eulogy for Vice Admiral Gordon McLintock
Fort Myer Chapel, Arlington, Virginia
April 30, 1990
Richard D. O'Leary

This is a day I have always avoided thinking about. I also never dreamed that I would be standing here for this purpose in this hallowed place. Muriel McLintock has honored me by asking me to offer some thoughts. But I did not know for sure that I could be here until a day ago. I wrote these notes on an airplane flying from Europe so they are in rough form, but my memories of the man are not.

I have decided not to talk about the Admiral's career and accomplishments in the Merchant Marine, Navy, and the Bureau of Marine Inspection, but only of the man, as I knew him.

He chose me to be his Aide and Assistant while I was still serving aboard the S.S. *United States*. I remember the interview and my first meeting with him on a snowy February morning. At the conclusion of that meeting, I knew that I had met an extraordinary man.

A few months later I joined him and sat for nearly three months in the same office with him and watched him work. This was his very unorthodox method of training me. I marveled at the range of his abilities and interests. And I probably laughed more during these months than during any other period of my life. He had the unusual ability to always inject humor into every situation no matter how serious or troublesome. And as all of you know, God blessed him with uncommon wit and a very sly lightning fast sense of humor.

At the end of this period I reluctantly moved to an adjacent office and continued to enjoy our relationship on a slightly less intimate basis. Kings Point was the centerpiece of his life and he and his wife Wynne served that Institution and its student body with all of their energy and the devotion of parents.

He was equally at ease with politicians, tycoons of Business or the upper hierarchy of the Clergy. He delighted in telling Senior Naval Admirals that John Paul Jones, Father of the American Navy, was a Scotsman and a Merchant Mariner like himself. His flair for public relations and his personal aplomb allowed him to accomplish miracles for the Academy during its earlier years of struggle. Anyone who is at all familiar with the history of the Academy knows that this man literally saved the Institution on a number of occasions.

It would not be appropriate nor could I do justice to a comprehensive listing of his accomplishments at the Academy. But highlights would certainly include: initial accreditation, creation of a magnificent

Chapel dedicated to the Merchant Marine dead of two World Wars, and management of the first Marine Nuclear Engineering program for the N.S. *Savannah* project. The beautiful grounds and buildings of Kings Point represent standing testimony to the skill with which this unusual man lead this Institution for more than two decades.

But his most important gift, as with all educators, lives on in thousands of men and women whose lives he touched. He constantly strove to inculcate in these sons and daughters of Kings Point a love for the sea, dedication to the seagoing profession, intellectual curiosity, Love of God, and pride in their Alma Mater. Their accomplishments and reputation are testimony to the success of his efforts.

I often wondered how this man would exist after the loss of his first wife and retirement, and if he would become a lonely recluse. I lost close touch with him for a while. When I again saw him, the answer was plainly obvious. He had existed just fine. He was as robust as ever with the same acerbic wit. His life was full of projects. He had many new friends. He was still the same elegant gentleman with more aplomb and grace than anyone I had met since I last saw him. But there was a grand new addition to his life, and her name was Muriel. They met and fell in love on a cruise off the coast of South America. I am convinced that this was not chance, but God's work.

I first met them together in the Norfolk Airport and his pride and love was shining in those twinkling blue eyes. My wife, Barbara, and I have shared some wonderful peak moments of life with them. They lived life in full measure. Joie de vivre radiated from both of them. Her talents as a painter, writer, conversationalist, and hostess fulfilled his passion for excellence. He referred to her as his "Sunshine" and I am certain that not only did she make his retirement delightful, but that she added years to his life. I know because he recently told me that the most disagreeable aspect of contemplating his mortality was the prospect of leaving Muriel.

As for me, I feel a little more alone than I did before last Monday. Admiral McLintock made me feel singular. He treated me as his son and I feel that whatever accomplishment I may have achieved somehow came about because of my association with him.

I have acknowledged privately to everyone and also in a good number of public speeches that he was my mentor. It is not so easy having a mentor, especially one that you love, because you have a tendency to periodically judge yourself by another person's standards.

He affected my life greatly. I brought my daughter Megan straight from the hospital to his house when she was born. My dogs have been named Magic after his poodle "Magic Mariner of Kings Point." Muriel's painting of Winslow Homer's *Breezing Up* is the focal point of our home on the Coast of Maine. I live with many joyful memories.

But I shall miss this man. I visited with him just two weeks prior to his passing, fully expecting to have a sad experience. Instead I found a man at peace, at peace with himself, at peace with life, a man at peace even with death, a man in love with his wife. To my surprise he asked me to have a Scotch with him. Incredulously I asked him, "Is this good for you?" and he said, "We will soon find out." It was the best Scotch of my life.

I asked him to repeat a favorite Scottish toast that I could never get straight. I did but I still cannot do it justice. I decided I would end these thoughts with that quote. I called Muriel from JFK Airport after coming from Europe. I asked her to repeat the quote. After hearing it I realized that it might be a little roguish for this moment. Still I am not so sure.

Author's note — This ending may seem a little abrupt, but there were only a few additional comments, and they did not really relate to Admiral McLintock.

RDO and Ami Vassiliades, President of Olympic Greek line.

Promoting Norfolk As Cruise Center

For a city whose lifeblood is shipping, Norfolk was slow to realize the potential of passenger travel.

Since the mid-1950's, when jets nosed out luxury liners as the primary means of traveling to Europe, cruise ships had turned their bows increasingly toward the Caribbean. Miami, cashing in on its proximity to this tourist mecca, quickly developed a cruise industry to rival New York's, yet Norfolk, between the two ports, was averaging only one sailing a year.

But in 1970, Richard D. O'Leary, then assistant general manager of the Norfolk Port and Industrial Authority, decided to actively seek out ship lines, market cruises and promote Norfolk as an embarkation point, something the local Chamber of Commerce had proposed without success, a decade earlier.

Later, he resigned his job and formed a company to market the idea. And in 1972, the first year O'Leary's Cruise International venture began chartering ships out of the port, there were 37 sailings, a number he considers remarkable because of the short lead time. Less than a year prior, he had managed to persuade Cunard Lines both to base its new ship, *Adventurer*, in Norfolk and to sail the pride of its fleet, the *Queen Elizabeth II*, from that port twice for long-duration cruises.

Through his additional efforts. Norfolk became home port for the Greek Line's flagship, *TSS Queen Anna Maria* and its *TSS Olympia*. Cruise International wholesales, books and promotes the vacation cruises to the islands of the Caribbean, a form of recreation and travel O'Leary feels is a "true bargain" about $55 a day. It also takes care of operations as stevedoring pier, planning and tug ordering.

A fourth of the tourists these cruises attract now come from Washington, 190 miles to the north.

By Claudia Levy

Norfolk Being Promoted As Embarkation Point

We're like a steamship company that doesn't own ships," he says, "and we're probably the only American company in that kind of business."

During the series of sailings that ended last week, the ships were averaging 500 passengers, about 200 under capacity, said O'Leary, 39, a former dean of students at the Merchant Marine Academy and former promoter for the U.S. Maritime Administration.

Norfolk the most nautical city in the country in O'Leary's view, and blessed with the "best natural harbor in the world," had always been a shipbuilding and docking center, both for the Navy, and for commercial operations. The port averages some 5,000 commercial sailings a year, and due in large part to O'Leary's efforts as a port administrator, has become second only to New York in the traffic of containerized cargo that can be easily transferred to freight cars and trucks.

It is O'Leary's dream to rebuild America's defunct ship line industry to rival the foreign cruise companies.

The luxury liner *SS United States*, where O'Leary once served as navigation officer, is docked at Norfolk while some use can be determined for it. Congress has forbidden its sale to a foreign country, mainly because of its major role in American shipping history. O'Leary has proposed that it sail to Europe in the summer and from Los Angles to Hawaii in the winter, carrying 3,000 passengers at $100 a head.

O'Leary, a native of Maine, has become a major booster of Norfolk, as well as its port. Early on, he says he had to work on local marine interests, city politicians, bankers, businessmen and others with influence to convince them that their city, long regarded as a conservative-and somewhat

apathetic-coal port and Navy town, was ripe for this kind of promotion.

He got the backing he needed, and the city pledged to spend $200,000 over the next three years advertising Norfolk as a cruise center. The port authority also agreed to refurbish its international terminals, scene of the embarkation of thousands of troops in World War II.

And with Williamsburg only 45 miles away. Norfolk could become a major tourist center, O'Leary said.

In a report commissioned by the port authority and recently released, retired Coast Guard Rear Adm. Irvin J. Stephens, a developer of the Port of Miami, recommends that Norfolk not strive to become a "second Miami in the cruise business." He cited several "limitations," including remoteness from the Caribbean and "lack of a 'magic' name." Some of his suggestions for promoting the cruise industry have already been undertaken, says O'Leary, who thinks that Stephens, "Like I do, has a bias" for his own city.

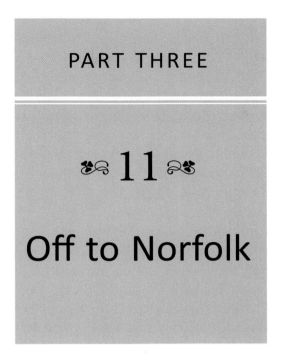

PART THREE

❧ 11 ❧

Off to Norfolk

 traveled down to Virginia for my interview with the Norfolk Port and Industrial Authority. I had been in Norfolk twice, each for a number of days, when I was on active duty with the Navy.

I really didn't know anything about the city itself, however. At first look it seemed to me there were areas of awakening in fields of blight. I learned the Port Authority operated the airport and Norfolk International Terminal, a large, deep-sea-ship terminal. In addition, it had bond-issuing authority, so there was also an industrial development responsibility.

As soon as I arrived I was subjected to an aptitude test and an IQ test. I later learned that I had scored the highest of anyone who took the IQ test. To my surprise, there was another candidate. We went to lunch together, which seemed a bit strange.

The board of directors was meeting at two o'clock. At one I met alone with the chairman, Mr. J. J. Gara, the person who had given me the rough invitation to come down. He said my record was good but that I was like a too-pretty girl, and I had held too many jobs. I explained that I had held only two besides the

81

Navy—at United States Lines and the Maritime Administration. He seemed somewhat mollified.

The interview with the board was rather routine, which I later learned was not always the case with this group. The general manager, a lovely man named Jim Crumbley, was smart, able, and hardworking. He had his hands full with many responsibilities. The chairman of this sometimes difficult board had an office on the premises. Jim Crumbley called a few days later to tell me I had the job if I wanted it. I accepted and agreed to start work in about a month, to give me enough time to settle my previously described pressing duties with the Maritime Administration. (This is an attempt at humor.)

I was invited to a dinner with the Virginia congressional delegation at the Marriott Hotel in Washington the night before I was scheduled to travel to Norfolk to start my job there. Also invited was a large group of Virginia business executives. I sat at a table with a group of them, none of whom I knew, and was dismayed by the conversation. Being a Yankee, and with no experience with Southerners, I was reminded sharply that I was going to a different part of the country. I'm not going to elaborate but there was one word used freely that I found offensive. It was extremely upsetting to me and I went home to my wife and expressed my great displeasure.

The next day I left in my MGB with a bit of a sad heart, wondering whether I had made a mistake. In addition, the idea of living for a couple of months, until school ended, without my children, in a rented room in a woman's private home, was not pleasant to contemplate. But by afternoon I was in my office on top of the Maritime Tower overlooking the great harbor of Hampton Roads. That evening I attended a reception as a guest of honor, along with a group of Belgian businessmen. The next day the lead story in the *Virginian Pilot* was about me. Things were looking up.

The authority was working on a number of major initiatives, among them the construction of a new airport and the development of the huge container terminal at Norfolk International Terminal.

There was also a small adjunct organization known as the Virginia Cruise Corporation. This was a quasi public-private corporation. It consisted of the commissioners of the Port Authority and some executives from the 21st Street Area Business Organization, a private business promotional group. The controlling vote rested with the Port Authority board. The purpose of the Virginia Cruise Corporation was to promote cruise-ship activity from the Port of Norfolk. The results of their efforts had been one cruise annually, known as the Virginia Cruise, in early January. It was usually on the *New Amsterdam*, a Holland America ship that sailed from New York, picked up passengers in Norfolk, and then sailed the Caribbean for two weeks.

Dealing with the authority's major issues was complicated somewhat by the board. It consisted of five commissioners appointed by the Norfolk City Council. They were all well-meaning and honest individuals, but the chairman was an irascible although lovable character who was continually maneuvering in the background trying to build little coalitions to control votes. One commissioner abstained on almost every vote of any importance. I suppose he thought this meant he'd never be caught on the wrong side of a vote in any future assessments.

Then there was a wonderful man who played an important role in my future. He was John Roper III, a graduate of the University of Virginia and MIT. The Ropers were one of Norfolk's old-time families. They owned Norfolk Shipbuilding and Drydock Corporation, one of the country's leading shipyards, and were the city's largest employer.

I participated in all the activities and concerns involving the authority. I took part in some controversies with success and seemed to attract a press following right from my earliest days there. For example, we had a problem with our police at the container terminal: they were aggressively searching longshoremen's cars for pilferage, including removing hubcaps. The situation worsened, with ever-increasing tension, and finally the longshoremen began throwing cargo into the water. In a bold move, I set up a committee of longshoremen leaders to police themselves. This was highly controversial, but it worked.

There was a huge controversy over building a new airport. There was a small group of activists who wanted to abandon the existing in-town airport and construct a brand-new facility in a place called the Dismal Swamp, over twenty miles out of town.

Being Irish, I must have had some verbal skills, which became recognized even by the mayor. Because of that talent, I suppose, I was selected to make a speech to the leaders of the six cities of Hampton Roads; their approval was necessary to get a key grant of federal funds. It passed, and was heralded in many newspaper articles, since these six cities agreed to support one airport.

Tom Mountjoy, a graduate of Virginia Tech and the University of Maryland's graduate program, developed the argument that made it possible. He was the first person I hired after coming to Norfolk. I mentioned earlier that I had achieved the highest score in the academy's admissions IQ test. I learned that later he beat me by one point. I always told him I had a hangover that day.

Back to the argument. He figured out that more than half of the people using the airport were Navy personnel, and the taxi fare to the proposed new location would more than double. This, along with other favorable facts, provided further inducement and won the day.

There were many other struggles, and General Manager Jim Crumbley was an expert in the airport business. Norfolk has a beautiful, efficient airport today thanks to his leadership.

Through my three years at the authority, I enjoyed a generally friendly press following. In fact, a wonderful reporter by the name of Cliff Hubbard, who was the maritime reporter of the *Virginian Pilot*, later sort of made a business out of writing about my activities for years. He even sailed from Warren, Rhode Island, two years later on our new *Spirit of Norfolk*.

The incidents outlined above are examples of some of things I became involved with. At the end of my first year, in 1970, the chairman of the authority invited me on the annual Virginia Cruise. Needless to say, I accepted. There were other guests aboard, including the mayor of Norfolk, Roy Martin. I enjoyed it tremendously, and started thinking about the potential of Norfolk as a cruise port. When I returned, I wrote a report outlining my ideas. It wasn't very difficult, as Norfolk had some very strong advantages. The report, more like a pamphlet, was mailed to the local press and the trade press, plus *Southern Living*, the *Richmond Times*, the *Washington Post*, and the executives of all of the cruise ship lines. Most were then located in New York City and Miami.

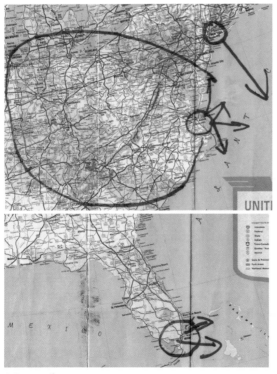

My market area map.

I was also offered the position of managing director of the Virginia Cruise Corporation, and I accepted it. Considerable interest was generated. I found myself speaking locally two or three times a week, and many weeks more often, both locally and out of town. I sent a barrage of mailings to the senior executives of all the cruise companies, enclosing specially prepared presentations and letters explaining the potential and advantage of Norfolk as the new mid-Atlantic cruise gateway. The promotional effort was so intense that one executive said, "I'll give you a ship if you'll just stop writing to me." This was followed by appointments and travel to meet with the executives. For many months I was on the road fifty percent of the time. It wasn't a question of one visit, but of many.

I used an ordinary map of the East Coast and drew a crude red circle around what I called the market area of the new mid-Atlantic cruise gateway. I also drew red circles around New York and Miami suggesting diminished market areas—a little exaggeration there.

The market area I depicted for Norfolk included Baltimore, Pittsburgh, and Cleveland to the north; Chicago, Cincinnati, Nashville, and Atlanta to the western and southeast perimeters; and Richmond, Norfolk, and Wilmington to the east. I carried the map with me on all my visits, and it drew an amazing amount of interest. Top executives would examine it as if it was a sophisticated market study. In some cases, executives would ask to copy it. I still have it after all these years.

The media took up the story. There were numerous articles in the Norfolk and Richmond papers. There were major articles in the *Washington Post* and some Virginia magazines. *Travel Weekly* and *Southern Living* magazines published articles about the promotional effort.

The trick now was to turn the interest into results. A number of companies seemed to be intrigued. I was wholly engaged in the project. I thought it was so important that it superseded my personal interests.

I wanted to have a strong inducement to attract these companies, so I wanted to create a promotional fund that would be used for joint advertising for the shipping company and the port. Between the port authority and the Visitor and Convention Bureau, we came up with a pool of 500,000 dollars.

In my judgment, the two leading prospects were Cunard Line and Greek Line, both of which were foreign companies. There were a number of others that looked promising as well. I really wanted only one company, in order to optimize the chances of a successful and prosperous operation in an untested market.

I became close friends with Richard Patton, the American president of the internationally known Cunard Line. He was a former vice president of Trans World Airlines and the number-two executive with the Campbell Soup Company. We developed a program that was beyond my wildest dreams. It was a bold and complex plan to pull off. Richard Patton was also going out on a long limb. We proposed that the great *Queen Elizabeth II* would do two pickup sailings of two-week cruises under the auspices of the Virginia Cruise Corporation, of which I was now managing director. The company would position its newest ship, then under construction in Norfolk, for its maiden summer season. The ship was the *Cunard Adventurer*, and it would undertake twenty-seven one-week cruises to Bermuda.

Before this was consummated, there was one important detail to contend with: I had to go to New York and make a presentation before the London-based Cunard Line board of directors, headed by Sir Basil Smallpiece.

I remember sitting on the steps of St. Patrick's Cathedral, on Fifth Avenue, and asking God to make this happen, not for me, but for the people of Norfolk. I guess it was successful, and the news was released to the press and the public. It created tremendous excitement in Virginia and in the cruise-ship and travel-agent industries. There was a huge reception for Cunard Line and the Norfolk business community. At the risk of sounding immodest, I was quite a popular guy.

I left with some of our staff, along with Dick Patton and some of his executives and personnel from Ogilvy & Mather advertising, to blitz the market. At this point I got to know a lot of the top executives from a number of cruise lines, and many are my friends to this day. I was even offered a very important job during this period.

Hampton Roads is an area made up of six cities: Norfolk, Virginia Beach, Portsmouth, Hampton, Newport News, and Suffolk. Norfolk was the historical urban center with the airport, Navy, and port facilities. Portsmouth and Newport News also had smaller port authorities. During the entire time I was there, there was talk of unifying the authorities into a state port authority. I even wrote some of the papers in favor of a state authority. I decided, however, that I didn't want to be an employee of the new authority. Because of my extensive training in business, my thoughts turned to the possibility of going out on my own.

When I first mentioned this to my father, he was adamantly opposed to such a proposition. He had been to Norfolk several times to see us, and I had sent him the many press clippings I had accumulated. He had stayed in the first modest house I had ever owned. Once again, he was worried.

I began to think about what I might do, and shared my thoughts with Tom Mountjoy and others. I also discussed some ideas with Jim Oliver, who was the public relations officer for the city of Norfolk. He's a fine person, a graduate of Notre Dame and Columbia University. We began having early-morning breakfast meetings once a week to brainstorm. I thought Jim would play a large role if we actually created a business, but this didn't happen. Jim went on to become the county manager of Williamsburg, the city manager of Norfolk for twelve years, and the city manager of Portsmouth. He actually did work with me for a short time years later between assignments. I tried to be circumspect, and never worked on my ideas on port authority time.

In our deliberations, lots of ideas were floated but my interest always centered on the cruise business. The result was that I was going to attempt to create a company.

Tom Mountjoy and I began to organize our thoughts and create a plan. I realized I would need an attorney and a CPA or finance person. We were joined by Charles E. Payne, an attorney, and Robert I. Low, a CPA with Goodman and Company. I stressed to them that the work would have to be done evenings and weekends and that there would be no pay.

We proceeded over a period of a number of months to formalize our plans, make financial projections, and prepare drafts of a confidential memorandum concerning the proposed organization of Cruise Ventures, Inc., a venture capital corporation.

In late 1971 I tendered my resignation to the authority. I explained that I wanted to continue the cruise-promotion activity, I hoped with private capital. Jim Crumbley, the general manager, graciously gave me a generous severance package. The chairman, however, was another story. I mentioned earlier that he was irascible but lovable. "I'll give you two choices," he said. "Within reason you can increase your salary and stay and I'll tear up your letter of resignation in front of the cameras. If you don't, I'll charge you with conflict of interest."

I replied that I had a letter from the city attorney saying that conflict of interest wasn't an issue. This was not pleasant, especially as it was the chairman who was really responsible for my coming to Norfolk. Of the two adjectives I used to describe him, I prefer the "lovable" because I did love him, and years later we reestablished a wonderful relationship that I treasured.

Suddenly I was on my own, and I felt something less than confident. Tom Mountjoy stayed on at the port authority. I now had to engage in capital formation, or, to put it more simply, I had to find some money.

I was depending primarily on being favorably known from the publicity that had accrued to me. We completed the final offering memorandum and I began calling on people to explain our plans. The people I called on generally had two characteristics—they were wealthy and well known. The memorandum described the plan and the personnel involved. It offered a package of stock for 5,000 dollars and a loan guarantee for 5,000, which I never had to call. This doesn't seem like much money today, but it was back in 1971.

I was offering twenty-five packages, of which I would purchase one. In turn I would receive fifty percent of the voting stock, which is called negative control, and the remaining fifty percent would belong to the other stockholders. No major action could be taken without agreement from at least one stockholder voting with the other block. It never came to that. At first I was encouraged; I sold some twelve packages in the early going. I also had the commitment of four prominent people, the mayor and three others who always invested together. That group fell through because of concern about a possible conflict of interest. At about the same time, my success rate slowed, and I wondered if I had made a serious mistake. With a family of three children, this would not be a good thing. This was not the last time I'd have this thought in the next few years. But sales did pick up and early in 1972 all twenty-five packages were committed. I was pleased about that, and also with the quality of people we had attracted.

I had simultaneously been negotiating with Dick Patton, of Cunard Line, and had a commitment for sailing the *Queen Elizabeth II* for January 1973, with our new little company handling the sales and marketing. The next step was to secure office space, which we did: four to five rooms in the windowless basement of an advertising agency owned by one of our new investors. My father visited at about this time and mentally contrasted it with my office in the Maritime Tower, and I knew he was quite worried.

On April 1, 1972, Cruise Ventures, Inc., doing business as (dba) Cruise International, was officially open for business. That launched what would be for me a thirty-four-year adventure.

THE CITY OF
PORTSMOUTH

Mrs. Barbara B. O'Leary
Vice President of Public Relations
CI Travel
101 W. Main Street, Suite 800
Norfolk, Va., 23510

Dear Barbara:

> *"Clap your hands, all you peoples; shout to God with loud songs of joy. "*
> *——Psalm 47*

Through Scripture I center myself to find words to celebrate Richard's journey to retirement. While I have only shared in parts of his life, those parts that I have shared have given me deep glimpses of his integrity, genius and steadfastness to serve thoroughly his God and the people around him.

My part of Richard's sojourn included his time with the Norfolk Port and Industrial Authority, the original grand pursuit of cruises for the port of Hampton Roads, founding of CI Travel, varied experiences as friend and adviser, and then service on his executive team. In those roles I felt the white hot part of the flame of his intense interest in the quest for breakthrough ideas or emotions as he sought to put forward the very best he could propose or cause to be put into action.

He rarely wilted from person or circumstance, in dogged pursuit of purpose. He never failed to find the last piece of unnecessary cost in a business proposal. Yet, though he is most comfortable being called a businessman, Richard dreams dreams beyond most mortals.

One truly wonders if Richard can retire if the word means give up, leave, quit, resign. My imagination says there is a chance for the second definition: become reclusive, cloister yourself, go away, go into retreat, retreat from the world, sequester yourself, withdraw. Certainly Richard is known to enjoy being by himself——as long as Barbara is nearby——as in Barbara, Barbara, where are you?

My wish for you, Richard, is the finish of a blessed life. You leave CI Travel with enormous distinction. You have been a wonderful, giving resident of our community.

> *"Go, eat your bread with enjoyment, and drink your wine*
> *with a merry heart; for God has long ago approved what you do. "*
> *——Ecclesiastes '*

Sincerely,

Jim Oliver

MARKETING *á la Carte*

THOMAS M VINCENT, Principal

April 2, 2005

At One With The Sea

It was Spring, 1970 and one of the busiest days ever at Ogilvy & Mather New York. Smack in the middle of it our advertising client Dick Patton, President of Cunard Line USA, called and said "Vincent, get over here right now. There's a guy from Norfolk making a case for the *QE2* to put in there on the way to the Caribbean this winter and I want to know what you think." In ten minutes, we were in Cunard's Conference Room, introduced to one Richard D. O'Leary of Norfolk's Port Authority and ready to listen. I was going to be hard to convince.

Mr. 0'Leary emphasized Norfolk's easy access to all of Virginia, North Carolina and beyond to West Virginia, D.C. and Maryland. He mentioned the great appeal the Cunard and *QE2* names would create in the region and the local pride cruise calls would engender. Then he talked about "the cruise experience" — the only true change of pace from a volatile, complex land-based world and the best possible place to adjust your attitude and reset your personal compass.

You could tell immediately he was zeroed in on the subject, loved what he was doing and wanted to spread the word. He was convinced his part of the world was just waiting with checks in hand for the right cruise ship to come along. We were more than impressed. We were sold!

That year, Norfolk's contribution to *QE2* sales was larger than the agreed on numbers. and more would come. This was really the prequel to the founding of CI Travel-Cruise International a few short years later. From that day on, our professional and personal relationship, sometimes with contact gaps of months or years, has remained intact and solid. We have worked together, traveled together, laughed together — even sung together. My regard for his field of vision and character, not to mention his humanity, knows no bounds.

He is "retiring" only in name. Benefits from his good works, creative imagination and zeal for competition will play on. His background interests and abilities tie him tightly to two great loves — Lady Barbara and the Sea - both wonderful anchors.

In tribute to both their achievements and with fond wishes for a bright future, perhaps Carl Schurz's words personify the unique O'Leary heritage best —

"Ideals are like the stars. We never reach them but, like the mariners on the sea, we chart our course by them."

Marketing á la Carte, Ltd.
25 Ingram Road, Briarcliff Manor, New York 10510
(914) 941-4107

12

The Adventure in Capitalism Begins

A very important first order of business was to establish a board of directors. The final board was from our investor group. Lee Payne, chairman of United Virginia Bank, was on the original board, but shortly after the first meeting, he resigned because our company was going to bank with his institution.

The board worked in harmony through several decades. It was a dedicated group made up of extraordinary individuals:

- Van Cunningham, chairman of the board, Stewart Sandwiches
- John Roper, president, Norfolk Shipbuilding and Drydock Corporation
- Jim Fishburne, president, Universal Products
- Charles Payne, principal, Payne, Gates, and Farthing
- Lee Payne, chairman, United Virginia Bank
- Bev Lawler, chairman, Lawler, Ballard, and Little Advertising
- Richard D. O'Leary, president, Cruise International

Here I'm all smiles, shortly after the opening of Cruise Ventures, Inc.

Now we had our team, and it was one that essentially stayed intact for more than thirty years. They were all wonderful people and worked together beautifully as a board.

LIFE LESSONS FROM MY FATHER AND OTHER PHILOSOPHERS

As we begin the story of the company, I would like to insert a rather personal section that pertains to my life and business philosophy, which I gleaned from others. That philosophy permeated how I managed the company.

Unknown Speaker, Webster Junior High School, Auburn, Maine

In the eighth grade a guest speaker from Alaska came to our school. He spoke eloquently about returning to his beloved Alaska and seeing the mountains rise out of the sea. The talk was very interesting, but there was one small portion that has had a huge impact on me throughout my life. He said, "The secret to success in life is to do a little more than people expect you to. You're bound to succeed because most people are trying to do a little less."

I've tried to make this my way of life. Everyone who has worked with me in my company is well aware that this is the company's philosophy as well as mine.

Organizational Dynamics

I'm not sure the Organization Dynamics company is still in existence, but at some point I learned of its work. It involved the principles of bottoms-up management. The idea is that the traditional business organization is turned upside down. A company should be operated so the people who interface with customers are on the flat top of a triangle, then there are layers of supportive people, until you reach the bottom point, which is where the CEO is located. At one time I had the company teach these principles to all of our people.

David Ogilvy, CEO of Ogilvy and Mather

David wrote a book called *Confessions of an Advertising Man*. I believe I speed-read this book. In talking about ad formation, he advocated that with every ad you should try to knock the ball out of the park. His number-two man, Tom Vincent, did much great work for our company and is a close personal friend.

Miss Murphy, Eighth Grade Teacher

Miss Murphy, my eighth grade Latin teacher at Webster Junior High School, often said, "Know where you are going before you are on your way." I have often repeated this in business meetings.

My Father

This was his personal code of behavior and I have tried to follow it, not always successfully:

1. Be good to everyone.
2. Honor thy father and thy mother.
3. Be good to your wife (my father was uxorious).
4. Love your family.
5. Try to do the very best you can, then let it go.
6. Do more than your share in matters of finance and life in general.

Personal Business Philosophy

The following is my personal business philosophy that I brought with me into this venture: With any success achieved, share it with two groups—the employees, and the people who believed and invested in you. I have tried to do this.

One of our early offices.

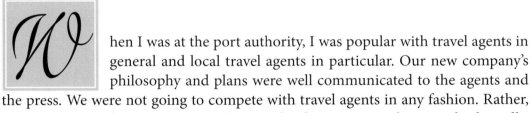

13

First Major Problem

When I was at the port authority, I was popular with travel agents in general and local travel agents in particular. Our new company's philosophy and plans were well communicated to the agents and the press. We were not going to compete with travel agents in any fashion. Rather, our plans called for us to support them with advertising, mailings, and sales calls. We would be acting as wholesalers and pay agents full commissions.

There were about forty travel agents in the Hampton Roads area. At the time, agents were selling the first two sailings of the *Queen Elizabeth II* through traditional methods—that is, by calling Cunard in New York to make reservations. We were introducing an almost unknown concept: a local company playing the role the shipping company normally filled. We thought this would work because of my background and also because of the concept of a local firm promoting a few sailings through travel agents.

In the group of forty travel agencies there was one called Mr. Happy Travel. This was a misnomer—Mr. Happy was anything but happy. In fact he became a zealot with the goal of putting us out of business. We received constant feedback about the things he was doing, such as making calls to all the agents and Cunard Line giving false and damaging information. He was successful in organizing most of the agents into a group called TATA (Tidewater Association of Travel Agents), ostensibly a promotional group. Early on we invited all the agents to a nice breakfast at a local hotel to make a presentation to them. The tables were set for about thirty agents who had responded favorably. When several of our key people and I arrived, we were surprised to see that only Mr. Happy and one other male agent were present. Mr. Happy was definitely not happy and let us know that the group was going to boycott us. We left with indigestion and a big bill.

It got worse. Our contract with Cunard was really based on my relationship with Dick Patton and his trust in me. The arrangement called for all reservations for our two *Queen Elizabeth II* cruises to be booked through our office so we could monitor and audit the results of our efforts.

Cunard Line had decided to move a company manager from the Pittsburgh area into the Norfolk market, primarily to promote the first two *Queen Elizabeth II* sailings and the twenty-seven sailings of the *Cunard Adventurer* in 1972. Our sailings were in January 1973. Mr. Happy asked the Norfolk manager if the agents could book our sailings directly through the company in New York. Because the manager was unaware of the special arrangements, he said yes. The TATA agents immediately booked reservations they had been accumulating through the New York office.

To paraphrase a cliché, "The ship was out of the barn," and I asked to be released from our contract with Cunard. It looked as if we would be out of business before we started.

Our little group huddled in the windowless basement in a state of despair. We had no ship and, therefore, no product to market. I decided to go back on the road and see if I could put something together.

The night before I left, I was at an intimate dinner at Tom Mountjoy's house. The atmosphere was more than bleak. Marilyn of Philadelphia was weeping and I couldn't offer any hope. It appeared that our little experiment in capitalism was probably a failure.

My first call in New York was to Jean-Claude Potier, the president of French Line, whom I knew from my port authority days. He was a charming man and I heard a number of charming stories, all told with a delightful French accent.

His company operated the *France* and, ironically, was headquartered in the same building as Cunard Line. He also made some vague reference to what he might be able to arrange. I was not hopeful. In fact, he actually scheduled one sailing of the *France* on his own, without us.

In those days the Port of Norfolk was similar to a crossroads with no gas stations. One opens and then there's one on all four corners. The number of sailings increased from one in 1971 to thirty-seven in 1972. It was a very competitive market for cruise ships.

I then traveled downtown to Canal Street and the headquarters of Greek Line. I already knew Ami Vassiliades, the executive vice president and CEO. He was a Greek and a Harvard graduate. John Goulandris's company owned two Greek Line passenger ships as well as a small fleet of tankers. I had met him in the past as well. Mr. Vassiliades and I examined the schedules of the *Olympia* and the *Queen Anna Maria*. I was seeking a program without financial risk, and we came up with an unorthodox program. We could have the *Olympia* for fourteen days in the early part of December 1972. This is traditionally the weakest time of the year for cruise marketing. The deal we eventually structured was along these lines. The *Olympia* carried roughly 750 passengers. The ship would be chartered to Cruise International for 20,000 dollars per day, for a total of 280,000 dollars. Greek Line would receive the first 100,000 dollars of collected revenue and we would issue a note guaranteeing the other 180,000 dollars. Under the terms of this quasi-charter, we would keep all the money above 280,000 dollars. This was actually more risk than I wanted to take and the possibility existed that we would be out of business. We entered into a contract.

The Olympia.

The Queen Anna Maria.

We decided to go with the philosophy of short and cheap, so we created two five-day cruises and one four-day cruise, all to Bermuda. The four-day cruise stopped in Bermuda for only about four hours. The cost was on average 50 dollars per person per day, allowing for a potential gross income of 525,000 dollars before travel-agent commissions of ten percent and the 280,000-dollar charter fee.

Along with the risk, however, was a very important advantage. Mr. Happy and TATA had to book passengers with us because the charter arrangement gave us control of the ship for the cruises.

In June we began a furious marketing campaign. Joining Tom Mountjoy and me, a character named Bruce Macswain served as vice president of sales. Bruce was his first name when he came aboard, but it kept changing—to Travis, River, and Brian, among numerous others. Every time he was deadly serious and I would pretty much ignore each change, until years later he came in with some official papers stating that his first name had been legally changed to Travis. In any case, he was a great VP of sales, and Travis, which I always considered a good name for a cowboy, turned out to be quite appropriate because since his retirement he has been roaming around the western mountains by himself. When I asked him once what he did out there he said, "I do a lot of hiking." When asked what was so special about that he said, "I hike naked except for cowboy boots." I told him I felt sorry for the animals.

For a company with ten or so full-time employees, we made a lot of noise in the market. On weekends we had people in malls in Norfolk, Richmond, and Washington. We struggled for free publicity promotions and trade deals. As we got closer to the cruise dates, we knew that although we had done quite well, we would not be able to fill the ships. When the sailing dates were imminent, we gave a lot of special deals to friends. Among ourselves we jokingly referred to the last sailing as a going-out-of-business sail. In between sailings, Greek Line sponsored a marvelous luncheon on the ship in Norfolk for about 350 people.

DailyBreak

ALBUM REVIEWS:
What the critics say about
Reba McEntire's "What If"
and other new releases/E3

She's the largest cruise ship the world has ever seen.
And at sunrise Friday, she'll be sailing into Hampton Roads.

A Date With Destiny

The Carnival Destiny at
sea: a $400 million
floating palace

CARNIVAL CRUISE LINE PHOTOS

BY STEPHEN HARRIMAN
TRAVEL EDITOR

A CARNIVAL is coming to our town Friday, a floating Carnival, the biggest Carnival you've ever seen. It's the Carnival Destiny, the biggest cruise ship ever built at 101,000 gross registered tons.

Because she's got things to do and places to go later in the day, Destiny will arrive in Hampton Roads with the sun. The turnaround in the Norfolk-Portsmouth basin of the Elizabeth River is scheduled for about 6:30 a.m.

Christened less than a month ago in Italy, she's on her way to her home port of Miami after promotional stops in Boston and New York.

She's coming here because Richard O'Leary, president of Norfolk-based CI Travel, told his friend Bob Dickinson, president of Carnival Cruises, "Hey, as long as you're passing here, why not let me see if we can put some paying passengers on board."

Not one but two overnight cruises were sold out almost quicker than you can say, well, "Biggest cruise ship ever built." With enough people left on a waiting list to fill another cruise. But that's not possible.

So, unless you have ticket in hand, all you'll be able to do is look her over from the shore.

Try to picture this as she glides down

Please see Destiny, Page E6

HOW BIG IS SHE?

M.S. CARNIVAL DESTINY
892 feet long

NIMITZ-CLASS AIRCRAFT CARRIER
1,092 feet long

The ship's
Palladium
Theater is
five decks
deep and
can seat
1,500. It
has a
Venetian
glass
chandelier.

Coming
aboard,
passengers
enter a
towering,
skylit
atrium
called the
Rotunda.

IF YOU WANT TO SEE HER

● Carnival Destiny is expected to arrive off Norfolk's Town Point Park about 6:30 a.m. Friday. It will turn around in the harbor and head for Newport News about 7:15 a.m.

● City of Newport News and Virginia Port Authority officials will welcome the Destiny at an 11 a.m. ceremony Friday at the north end of the Marine Terminal, upriver from the coal piers.

● Cruise 1 will depart at 5 p.m. Friday and return at 6:30 a.m. Saturday. Cruise 2 will depart at 5 p.m. Saturday and return at 6:30 a.m. Sunday. Both cruises are sold out.

● The Destiny will depart Newport News for Miami about 10 a.m. Sunday.

● The Spirit of Norfolk will offer an escort tour Friday, and Newport News Harbor Cruises will have a breakfast viewing cruise Sunday. Call 627-7771 for information on the Spirit or 245-1533 for the Newport News tour.

MAP ON PAGE E6

In 1996 this was the biggest ship in the world.

✥ 14 ✥

A New Beginning

On the return to Norfolk from the last Greek Line cruise, I noticed reporters on the pier. I soon learned that Cunard was not going to return the *Cunard Adventurer* to Norfolk in 1973. The buzz concerned whether we could get Greek Line to fill the void. I tried to create the illusion that I would talk to Greek Line, but I would be talking with other lines as well.

Greek Line was delighted with the results we had achieved with the three sailings. We made just a small amount above the charter cost. Greek Line made much more than it ever had in New York during these early December dates.

Ami Vassiliades had seen what we could do and wanted to come to Norfolk, but not without us. He offered us a good program of sixteen cruises. Of greatest importance, there would be no guarantee by us and Greek Line would accept no bookings in New York. We were off; there was jubilation in the windowless basement and great discontent in the offices of Mr. Happy.

He didn't stop trying to do us harm, but TATA was finished. We lost a little money in our first year, but that was the only time in the next thirty-three. Ami

Toasting a new beginning with Tom Mountjoy (left) and Travis Macswain (right).

Vassiliades was a great friend to our company and defended and saved it twice. I believe he now lives in Greece.

The next year was quite successful and Mr. Vassiliades diverted more sailings from New York. Greek Line also had a similar general-agency agreement in Boston for many years. He took sailings from the Boston operation and gave them to us in Norfolk. After two years of this, the owner of the company in Boston decided to retire. I proposed that our company take over the Boston operation and Greek Line agreed. We now had Cruise International offices in the Park Plaza Hotel and about ten new employees, led by Barbara Varley. This especially pleased me because of my New England background. I was particularly fond of an old Irishman named Arthur Donovan, who reminded me of my father. He called on agents and I allowed him to do pretty much what he wanted to. Years later, he was only working part-time, and I paid him even when he no longer came in.

Our air charter business continued to grow. We opened a shopping center location in Hampton, Virginia. It was not a typical travel agency but rather a travel superstore. In addition to agents and routine service, it housed a film theater, a store that sold travel-related items such as luggage, and a reading room with newspapers from all over the world. This was a prototype that we hoped to rapidly expand. It was exciting but it didn't work. Although this office survived, the concept didn't. We began expanding instead with traditional offices, first in Virginia and then in other locations.

Nothing stays the same. In 1975 Greek Line was experiencing financial difficulties. This was a difficult period for the cruise industry in general. It was well known that a number of lines were in trouble. The *Queen Anna Maria* was sailing for us from Boston and Norfolk. We noticed slow payment of our stevedore bills, which is for longshoremen labor. One morning I woke up to learn that the *Queen*

Anna Maria had left New York in the middle of the night for Greece. I received a phone call from the company telling me that Mr. Goulandris wanted to see me in New York. I only went because I was hoping for some good news.

I went up there and met with Mr. Goulandris and Mr. Vassiliades. About the only thing said of any substance at the meeting came from Mr. Goulandris. He said, "Deek, I've decided to lay up the ships." That fact was apparent; it was the talk of the New York waterfront and the whole shipping industry. It was not a pleasant flight back to Virginia. A short time later I heard that they left in the middle of the night with the permission of their creditor, a large New York bank.

I was back in my customary position of looking for a ship. But this time I had some actual business in the form of deposited groups in Boston and Norfolk, so I inflated the numbers a little and began again. Maurice Zarmati, an employee of a new company called Carnival Cruise Lines, practically lived in our offices. Because of him, I used to get phone calls from its vice president of sales, Bob Dickinson. I later described these calls as being like a hand coming out of the phone and putting a stranglehold on my neck.

We had a group of about 600 Shriners expecting to sail from Norfolk on Greek Line in September. Carnival had one ship, called the *Mardi Gras*, and it had suffered a bad start, including running aground off Miami on the maiden voyage. The story goes that they were taking money out of the bar cash registers to pay for fuel.

We both had needs but they were different. They were trying to get a Miami operation going and we were trying to get ships for Norfolk and Boston, not send customers to Miami.

We worked out a deal. We would send our Shriners to Miami in June, and Carnival would give us a cruise in Norfolk and one in Baltimore in September in conjunction with the annual shipyard overhaul in Norfolk. The cruises were more than successful; they were blowouts. I think we even overbooked them. That's rare.

So both of our companies survived and that was the beginning of a long-term business relationship. It also began a long-term personal relationship with Ted Arison, the owner of Carnival; Micky Arison, his son; and Bob Dickinson.

The company has gone on to become the largest cruise ship company in the world, owning many lines including Cunard. I believe it now owns more than half of all cruise ships. Ted Arison, who has passed away, is regarded by me as one of the greatest entrepreneurs who ever lived; Micky is now chairman. Bob Dickinson became president of Carnival Cruise Lines and we are still very close with him and his wife, Jodi.

The business relationship went on for many years and we enjoyed a secure profit center.

CARNIVAL
CORPORATION & PLC

BOB DICKINSON
President
Chief Executive Officer

Mr. Richard O'Leary
101 W. Main Street, Suite 800
World Trade Center
Norfolk, VA 23510

Dear Richard,

I find myself unusually emotional as I contemplate all that you've meant to me over these last 31 years:

You have been and continue to be my best male friend. You have been at various times, my business counselor, stock broker, career analyst. And, at other times: my father, brother or son.

- o You have an incredible *joie de vivre* that inspires me and elevates all those who have the pleasure of your company. From the Combat Zone to the Caribbean, from Venice to Naples, from Maine to Miami…some of my most joyous moments on earth have been in your company.

- o And, you have had the great good fortune and extraordinary wisdom to marry above your station!

- o On this day of retirement, please take great joy and pride in your extraordinary business achievements which have enriched the lives of so many people.

May you continue to enjoy, inspire and love…for many, many years to come.

         Bob

RDO and Bob Dickinson, president of Carnival Cruise Lines, in 1975.

The cruise business remained a mainstay of our company for decades. We developed a unique business. Our reputation grew as a company able to produce significant revenue in the off-seasons, when business in New York and Miami was slowest. We learned to market the weaker ships at the worst times of year.

We also took the business to other ports. We operated out of Norfolk; Baltimore; Philadelphia; Wilmington, North Carolina; and Charleston, South Carolina. Our reputation usually enabled us to get ship programs without chartering; we used a general-agency agreement instead. We did charter two other times when market conditions forced us to do so in order to maintain continuity of our programs. One was the *Caribe*, owned by Commodore Cruise Line. We sailed the ship from Norfolk and Boston.

Years later, in 1996, my new wife, Barbara, and I were invited to Venice for the launching of Carnival Cruise Lines' new ship, *Destiny*. At the time, it was the largest cruise ship in the world. We were included in a group of about twenty-five special guests of Carnival who stayed on the ship for three days.

Ted Arison, Micky Arison, and Bob Dickinson were in the party. Lynn Arison, sponsor and wife of the owner, launched the ship with a bottle of champagne.

To create interest, the ship was going to make two daylong stops in Boston and New York. I suggested to Bob Dickinson that we'd be willing to charter it and put some paying passengers on it. We worked out a beneficial charter rate and scheduled it out of Newport News, Virginia, for two one-night cruises to nowhere. The plans generated enormous publicity. Newspapers called it a "Date with *Destiny*." Bookings came into our offices so fast that we were constantly raising the prices during the short time tickets were available. We moved more than 6,000 people at extraordinarily high rates.

The Mardi Gras.

TRADITIONAL HARBOR WELCOME BY TUGS AND FIRE-
BOATS GREETS THE BRAND-NEW 20,000-TON CRUISE
SHIP M/S SEA VENTURE OF FLAGSHIP CRUISES,
INC., AS SHE SAILS PAST THE BATTERY ON HER
MAIDEN ARRIVAL AT NEW YORK CITY, MAY 27, 1971

The Sea Venture.

The Caribe.

The Kungsholm.

The Carnivale.

The Olympia.

Among the lines whose ships we worked with over the years were Carnival, Greek Line, Home Lines, Celebrity, Bahamas Cruise Lines, Cunard Line, and Paquet. Since the inception of the company we brought twenty-six ships from sixteen cruise lines just to Norfolk. We had established a unique and profitable niche business.

Four new and talented people joined our executive team. Kevin McElroy, an excellent man, headed the travel agency division and Jim Denton ran our military division, flying planeloads of Navy dependents to the Mediterranean. He was also an all-purpose executive and perhaps played the role of the son I never had. Coe Sherrard was head of the *Spirit* division. Joe Good, who rounded out the team, headed the military commercial travel division. This involved supervising the commercial travel of a number of military bases, which we had acquired in national competition with other agencies. Mickey Hawks joined us as head of the retail travel division. She is a wonderful person and made invaluable contributions to the growth of the company. Then Steve Coplon worked his way up through the accounting department to become comptroller and ultimately director of special projects. He had a knack for coming up with exactly the numbers I wanted when evaluating new business opportunities; that means optimistic and sometimes not realistic.

It was in this period that two important and terribly sad events occurred. The first was the death of my father, on May 15, 1974. At age eighty-four he was still carrying out the trash barrels for two women who had apartments in his building in Haverhill, Massachusetts, to which he had moved himself from Auburn with a little truck. He had been a fine specimen of a man; no nursing home for him.

There's one special experience with him that I'll never forget. In his last year I went to visit my parents for just an overnight. As soon as I arrived he said, "It's very important that you take a short walk with me." When we started down a hill past Haverhill's YMCA, I noticed that he was walking quite fast. He was always proud of his walking ability and I realized that he was showing me he could still do it.

We ended up at the drugstore where he purchased his medicine. He took me over to the pharmacist and asked him, "What do you think of my boy?" I was in my early forties and was looking for somewhere to hide. The pharmacist looked at me quizzically and said, "He seems very nice."

In his last six months my father had been having slight fainting spells, each lasting about fifteen minutes. The doctor said it was due to narrowing of the arteries in his neck. I was on active naval duty up in the mountains of Virginia when my sister Arlene called and said he had suffered one of these spells and was in the hospital. This put me in a terrible position because we were near the end of the two-week exercise and I was slated to be the presenter. I kept calling to see if he was dying and they kept telling me no. And then I got a call on the next to the last day that he had died. I was shattered.

I drove to Norfolk and caught a plane to Boston. I stood at the head of his casket during all the visiting hours. I came across this poem that captures the essence of what I was feeling.

Father and Son

Only last week, walking the hushed fields
Of our most lovely Meath, now thinned by November,
I came to where the road from Laracor leads
To the Boyne river—that seems more lake than river,
Stretched in uneasy light and stript of reeds.

And walking longside an old weir
Of my people's, where nothing stirs—only the shadowed
Leaden flight of a heron up the lean air—
I went unmanly with grief, knowing how my father,
Happy though captive in years, walked last with me there.

Yes, happy in Meath with me for a day
He walked, taking stock of herds hid in their own breathing;
And naming colts, gusty as wind, once steered by his hand,
Lightnings winked in the eyes that were half shy in greeting
Old friends—the wild blades, when he gallivanted the land.

For that proud, wayward man now my heart breaks—
Breaks for that man whose mind was a secret eyrie,
Whose kind hand was sole signet of his race,
Who curbed me, scorned my green ways, yet increasingly loved me
Till Death drew its grey blind down his face.

And yet I am pleased that even my reckless ways
Are living shades of his rich calms and passions—
Witnesses for him and for those faint namesakes
With whom now he is one, under yew branches,
Yes, one in a graven silence no bird breaks.

—F. R. Higgins

I first went to Ireland with a group of travel executives about two years after my father died. I was staying in Jury's Hotel in Dublin and went down to see a cabaret show. The first song they played was "Danny Boy." I wept. It's a hauntingly beautiful melody, maybe the most famous in the world. The English lawyer and lyricist Frederick Weatherly wrote the song in 1910, the same year my father arrived in America. The lyrics were originally written for a different tune. Weatherly modified them to fit the classic "Londonderry Air" in 1913.

There's some question about whether this is a message from a woman to a man or vice versa. I've always heard that it was from a man to a man. It has also been interpreted as a message from a parent to a son going off to war or leaving as part of the Irish Diaspora. "Diaspora" is an unusual word that means dispersal. The potato famine around 1850 caused the country to lose much of her population. The melody is reported to be the most popular of the twentieth century. When I listen to these words, I know from his knowledge of the characteristics of the elements and the nature of the terrain that the writer spent some time in Ireland. Every time I hear the song I become emotional and miss my father all over again. Here are the words to the second verse of "Danny Boy":

But when ye come, and all the flowers are dying,
If I am dead, as dead I well may be,
Ye'll come and find the place where I am lying,
And kneel and say an Ave there for me;
And I shall hear, though soft you tread above me,
And all my grave will warmer, sweeter be,
For you will bend and tell me that you love me,
And I shall sleep in peace until you come to me!

His death occurred when the company was two years old. He followed everything I did. He traveled to Virginia by bus a couple of times and was aware only of the early struggles. He carefully read all the newspaper clippings and he worried. I think I inherited some wonderful traits from him, but I too am a worrier and adhere to that old adage "Expect the best but plan for the worst." It must be of Irish derivation.

What is incredibly sad for me is that he never saw any of the signs of the success that was to come. He didn't see the ships, the vast growth of the airline and travel businesses, and the waterfront headquarters building. He never saw the symbols of personal success: multiple beautiful homes, yachts, respect, and a wonderful and satisfying family life.

The second major event is that my marriage ended in divorce. I don't think it is a compliment to me that it happened when I was home rather than when I was on a ship. I've been facetiously calling her "Marilyn of Philadelphia," but I want to make it clear that she is a fine woman. She bore me three beautiful daughters and was and is a wonderful mother to them. On the day our divorce was finalized, I wept. I offered her a trip to Hawaii, but she declined it. Over the years we've become friends and spend time with our daughters on holidays. She has even attended our annual Fourth of July extravaganza at our home in Maine.

CRUISE INTERNATIONAL

Spirit Harbor Cruises
CI Travel Centers
Cruise International Ocean Cruises

15

Group
Business

We introduced a new strategy for developing group business. We had personnel doing nothing but soliciting groups. We completed a full-color group cruise guide, produced by Tom Vincent of Ogilvy & Mather, and presented it as an informational guide rather than a sales piece. The strategy involved getting groups committed for the future so we could use them as a base to schedule cruises. Part of the strategy was to put ads in newspapers that were pictures of the pamphlet itself. One of the respondents was a large national insurance company, in Hartford, Connecticut. They were interested in a major anniversary party involving more than 3,000 people. We arranged to charter Holland America's *Rotterdam* for two voyages. The charters were signed after much work. I spent a good deal of time in Hartford. Much to my great disappointment, a company attorney, while at a legal convention, discovered that New York State insurance laws prohibited this type of event. There were no tax advantages allowed. I lobbied Governor Hugh Carey of New York, who had been on our Congressional Advisory Board at Kings Point, but to no avail. This was a huge blow for a young company.

We had commitments, though, including a number of Virginia associations. We moved the Virginia Association of Realtors, the Virginia State Bar, the Virginia Nurses Association, and many more. Each of these groups had hundreds of members. We put into effect our base strategy of giving them excellent service and doing more than they expected. All of the organizations had one thing in common: none had ever left the state for a convention. In fact, they were prohibited by their bylaws from doing so. We became experts in how to help them accomplish getting around this.

The cruises were all quite successful. The members liked cruising and they liked leaving the state, but they didn't want to cruise twice in a row, so we entered the air business. At first we chartered planes only for the groups we developed. But then we began selling air packages to the public through a vehicle called ITC (Inclusive Tour Charter). It was against the law for a company to sell air transportation directly to the public. ITC required a package that was comprised of three stops.

We soon were marketing ITCs to Hawaii and California. We continued chartering planes for groups. We chartered two 747s out of Washington to Puerto Rico for the Virginia State Bar.

Federal law had prohibited direct sales to the public by travel promoters. After the law was changed, we ran weekly planes to Las Vegas, rotating them from Washington, Raleigh, North Carolina, Richmond, and Norfolk. We now had three profit centers.

Because we had dabbled successfully with air, we took another step. In those days travel agents would offer travel services to companies for their employees' business travel. Because of limited capital, they would bring a bill to be paid when the tickets were delivered.

I knew most of the heads of good-sized businesses in the Norfolk area and mounted a campaign offering them once-a-month billing. We quickly became the biggest commercial company in the city, and have remained so to this day. In fact, we took this business far and wide, operating in twelve states, including Hawaii and also Washington, D.C. Some of the biggest accounts were NASA; a number of huge airbases, including Wright-Patterson Air Force Base in Ohio and Patrick Air Force Base in Florida; and the Security and Exchange Commission. Thus, the business we began with Norfolk companies was our fourth and a rapidly expanding profit center.

During this period, we became involved with the author of a number of well-known handbooks for economical travel in Europe right after the Second World War. He not only wrote books but was also a raconteur extraordinaire. Our first association with him came about because of Barbara's very successful annual travel show. We engaged him to do some lectures as one of its features. The lectures were about two hours long and were received very well. He could speak for hours, nonstop, everything interesting and entertaining. We learned a little later that he was doing network TV commentary and also creating actual travel programs.

He called one day and told me about a program he was putting together. It involved flying chartered planes to Orlando. The package price covered airfare, hotel room, land transfers, and admittance to Epcot. The Disney attraction was so new that I had never heard of it.

As always, the writer spun a wonderful tale of profits, satisfied customers, and incredible potential. He asked us to join him as a wholesaler. We agreed to take on the promotion of several cities, among them Washington, D.C. It sounded wonderful and we put together a promotional program with excitement and high expectations. Coe Sherrard, who had managed many of our successful *Spirit* programs, was the executive in charge.

The operation began with much fanfare and an expensive advertising blitz. Early feedback was less than good. In fact, it was bad and got worse. The planes were often badly off schedule, buses at Disney failed to show up, and people arrived and found they had no hotel reservations. Also, instead of a nonstop flight to Orlando, planes were often diverted to other cities to pick up passengers, making the trip more grueling and usually very late.

Coe, a meticulous manager, was getting increasingly frazzled. He would tell me this program was going to ruin our hard-earned reputation and all we had worked for. We were not the program's operator, so any attempts to remedy the problems had to be made through our friend, the talented promoter.

Coe assured me that he had been continuously working on this and it was hopeless, so we needed to end our involvement. He finally convinced me this was our only sensible course of action. I agreed to make the phone call.

I dialed with Coe sitting nervously at my side. I got the great promoter on the phone and as usual he took over the conversation. The conversation went on for a long time with only short interruptions from me. He explained that there were the usual startup problems but they were being eliminated. He had a reasonable answer for every problem I pointed out.

It must be understood that this man is one of the world's most articulate speakers. The call finally ended and Coe asked what had happened. I told him with some amount of embarrassment that we had taken on two more cities—Hartford and Providence.

I'm not proud of it, but at least the situation didn't last too long, and we were soon out of the Epcot business. This was only temporary, however; after some time, we marketed a similar program on our own and it was a success.

My Barbara

y personal life changed dramatically. I did some dating, and had a relationship for over a year, although we never lived together, with a nice person who was much younger than I.

There was a beautiful woman, named Barbara, who appeared on local television. She cohosted a one-hour live talk show and also taught exercise and yoga. She was quite the rage in Tidewater, Virginia. I later learned that not only was she married but she had four daughters as well—Michele, Stephanie, Danielle, and Dione. I rarely saw her on morning television, but I appeared on her show a number of times. I agreed with the consensus that she should be on national TV. I also did yoga for much of my life, but not on television, thank goodness.

Our company used her in promotional TV spots for cruises. She then moved to Washington, D.C., with her husband. He was a successful naval aviator who had been shot down in Vietnam and made a heroic escape. He has since been selected for flag rank.

Some years went by and I learned that she was back in Hampton Roads, with her children, and legally separated. She was producing short TV film pieces and our company was one of her customers.

As these stories go, we met and began seeing each other. I knew almost immediately that I had met my soul mate. We had a wonderful relationship and that included our seven daughters. We saw each other for more than three years, although we never lived together, and our daughters got along well with each other.

During this period she said she would like to work for our company. This was a lucky day for the company because she went on to play an invaluable role for more than thirty years, in a number of capacities.

She worked in sales and managed the group department. She started a newsletter called *The Traveler*. She created an annual innovative travel show that was reputedly the second biggest in the country. Nobody told her travel shows had to be dull, so she had food and live entertainment and created a carnival-like atmosphere. Later she successfully sold cruises and travel packages at the show, against my better judgment. She had about forty agents equipped with computers and they sold hundreds of thousands of dollars in travel every day. She eventually became the decorator, and then the head of construction, for our 600-passenger harbor cruise-ship fleet. Of equal importance, she was one of the most respected employees. She was a friend and confidante to all, and was a beloved figure.

Barbara O'Leary (right) at the christening of the Spirit of Norfolk *with Shirley Leafe, wife of the mayor of Norfolk.*

With Barbara in the owner's suite of the Millennium, *a new Celebrity Line ship.*

I was satisfied with our relationship, but we were on the cover of *Metro*, a regional magazine, with a big story that pointed out that we weren't married. She said she was embarrassed and that we needed to do something.

Some of my friends questioned my sanity for even thinking about marrying someone with four daughters when I had three of my own. I suspect she received some warnings also. We did it anyway.

In preparation, Barbara went to five months of religious training, and I accompanied her. We met Father Vince Connery, a young priest who changed our lives. Barbara became a Catholic, and went on to be the first convert and the first female to become president of Sacred Heart Church in Norfolk.

We were married on May 24, 1980, in the presence of our seven daughters. I want to take this opportunity to say that this was the greatest decision I ever made. Barbara has created a wonderful family. In particular, she has made these seven girls truly love each other. I take little credit for this; she works at it all the time.

She is the most beautiful, most joyful, loving, thoughtful, patient, caring person I've ever known, a grand example of God's work.

This is a rather silly little thing I wrote a few years after we were married. Barbara has kept it, along with the picture, framed all these years.

> I don't know where I was on March 3 in the seventh year of my life. Riding a tricycle on Pulsiver Street I suppose.
>
> I do not even now know the time it happened on that day. However, I suspect that at that very moment I experienced an unexplained wave of exhilaration.
>
> If I had known it was the moment you were born, I know I would have got off my tricycle or stopped whatever I was doing and applauded.
>
> I also know that all the happy moments of those 38 years would have been a little happier, and the sad moments a little less sad because of the anticipation of you.
>
> I shall forever be grateful to two people from Iowa.

17

Our Canine Family

ogs have played an important part in our lives. Barbara and I equally love them and spoil them, and a number of people have told us they'd like to come back in the next life as an O'Leary dog.

When I was a child, we had a number of mongrel dogs, all of whom I loved, and lots of cats. That means we also had many litters of kittens, which I also loved. The sad aspect here is that those litters would periodically disappear. I learned later that it was my father who made them disappear. Otherwise, I guess we'd have been overrun with cats.

There was a long period, during my educational and seagoing years, when I lived without animals. Marilyn of Philadelphia had little interest in pets, like none.

When I lived at the U.S. Merchant Marine Academy, my mentor, Vice Admiral McLintock, had two standard black poodles, a father and son. I had never thought much of poodles and regarded them as froufrou dogs. This pair was basically taken care of by two stewards. Every once in a while, the younger one, Magic

Mariner of Kings Point, got loose and I'd see him galloping around the academy grounds. He looked like a magnificent stallion to me.

After I married Barbara, things changed. First of all, she came with an old Great Pyrenees dog named Shiva, who lived for less than a year.

Then at a Naval Reserve meeting, one of the members had a litter of Irish setters he was giving away. I took one and presented him to Barbara's children. We named him Irish, and he turned out to be less than perfect. His favorite pastime was to dig large holes around the foundations of buildings. He also had an annoying habit of jumping onto the backseat of my new car, doing his business, and then working fiercely to get out. When he was about a year old, I received a call in my office from Danielle, who told me Irish had run away. She was hysterical. She said she and her sisters had put up reward signs all around the neighborhood. She also told me they had called various SPCAs and thought they found him at the one in Norfolk, about eighteen miles away. She begged me to leave immediately to retrieve the dog. In spite of the fact that I was in an important meeting, I left. There was an Irish setter but it turned out to be a female with missing teeth who'd recently had puppies. I relayed the bad news to Danielle. She thought a moment and then said, "Bring her anyway." I didn't, so we were once again dogless.

Sometime later we were thinking about finding another dog and I remembered Magic Mariner of Kings Point. We began a search for a poodle, and found one in Kennebunkport. She was a one-year-old black standard, a beautiful and spirited animal. She belonged to Leslie and Carl Lindgren and their children, Jessica and Eric. They were forced to give her up because Jessica was experiencing some health problems. The poodle's name was Lindy and she became a centerpiece of our lives. She lived with us, traveled with us, and, most importantly, sailed with us for thirteen years. She was such a source of joy that I wrote this little piece about her after she died. We've remained close with the Lindgren family, and they've come to our Fourth of July celebration every year since we obtained Lindy.

All of our daughters have dogs. Four of them have poodles, unsolicited gifts from us. The other three have various breeds, some of them adopted and saved.

Barbara bought me another black female poodle from a pet store in Naples, Florida. Actually, "bought and saved" would be a more accurate description. We think she had a rough upbringing as a puppy in Cincinnati. She didn't have quite the lineage of Lindy. She was a bit crazy, in fact, but we came to love her anyway and named her Lindy II.

Lindy I on McGlathery Island in Maine.

Lindy Lou

How long has it been since you left us?
I hear sounds and I think it is you.

At times when I turn my head quickly I think I see you.
I walk the streets where we walked together and I miss you.

I do not feel the rain now and never minded the elements when you walked with me.
I do absurd mental calculations such as how many times you rode the elevator.

Our beautiful boat seems strangely different without you.
People who are unaware sit in your place in the cockpit not knowing it was your spot.

There are so many firsts without you.
We soon drive to New York for the first time without our companion.

Soon we will be where you came from—home in Maine but without you.
Our little core family of three has been badly torn, and I resent it.
But then I think of the joy you gave us.

You were a sailor dog, a people dog, and a regal lady, and I realize how fortunate we
were to have been with you all of those years.

Perhaps there will be another beautiful black animal in our life—but not now.

I suspect that you are somewhere where you are happy, and that you are well now.
I would imagine that you look like you did the first time I saw you,
glorious in the sun of a summer day in Kennebunkport.

We will soon spread your ashes in the places you have known and loved,
And we will never forget you.

Lindy II, Sophie, and Lucy enjoying Venetian Bay in Naples, Florida, on our Hinckley picnic boat.

Three years ago, Barbara ordered a poodle for Danielle, who lives in New York, as a birthday present. She was going to drive to Gray, Maine, to pick up the dog. We had planned to enjoy the puppy for about a month before presenting it to Danielle. Because of my dog mania, I volunteered to accompany Barbara to Gray, Maine. There we met this gorgeous white poodle puppy, the one destined to be the gift. I was walking around looking at the other dogs and saw a black-and-gray, unusual-looking puppy walking around by herself. I said to Barbara, "Let's get another one for us."

We headed home with Lindy II, who was nine, and the two little ones. We came to enjoy and love them so much that we couldn't separate them. We even sold two condominium homes so we could keep them together because three dogs weren't allowed. One was our condominium in Norfolk, the other was a condo in Florida. So we now have three poodles: Lindy II, Sophie, and Lucy. Danielle now owns two "New York" Labradors named Hudson and River.

I'm sure Danielle loves the Labs but Barbara and I idolize our poodle family. Because of our former work in travel, we used to fly first class all over the world. This, combined with the ability to cruise anywhere and at any time, made for a very enjoyable lifestyle. We're now relegated to a life of permanent dog

RDO and BBO with Lindy II at Belgrade Lakes.

sitting and seasonally driving our dogmobile up and down the East Coast, but we couldn't be happier.

Author's Note — I am very sorry to say that as this memoir was being completed we lost Lindy II. There is much sadness in the O'Leary household.

Introduction of first Spirit of Norfolk *to Norfolk, Virginia.*

PART FOUR

❧ 18 ❧

The First
Spirit

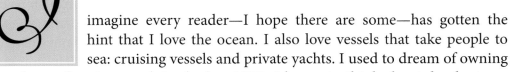

imagine every reader—I hope there are some—has gotten the hint that I love the ocean. I also love vessels that take people to sea: cruising vessels and private yachts. I used to dream of owning some form of cruise vessel. In the late 1970s I began to think about developing a vessel and a product that would compress the elements of a one-week ocean cruise into a three-hour experience.

All of the major harbors in the United States had some kind of harbor cruise, but there were none of any consequence. There were booze cruises, and some major sightseeing operations, such as the Circle Line in New York. Most of these boats were a lot less than sophisticated, however.

I engaged our executive group in brainstorming how we could implement a plan to develop a cruise with the compressed elements of a one-week cruise. The first component didn't require much serious thought—we needed a vessel.

I looked in trade publications for a small ship that would lend itself to this purpose. I found an ad for a vessel in Michigan that sounded interesting. It was laid up but had been used as a tourist attraction in a Detroit theme park. I flew out there with Tom Mountjoy. In the airport I had a copy of a brochure for the *Carrie B*, a Norfolk operation. I drew an X through the *Carrie B*. This was a bit premature, especially as we had previously tried to buy that ship and were turned down. When we first saw the Detroit boat, we realized it wasn't a thing of beauty, to say the least, but it was a small ship. It was old but it was big, about 250 feet long. It was built in 1941 for the Navy as an LCI (landing craft infantry), carrying 191 troops and their equipment. I later learned that it had made two trips to and from Africa and was not expected to return each time. These were designed as dispensable vessels.

She still had 1941 equipment and technology in her. She was advanced for 1941 but not adequate for the 1970s. She had been licensed by the U.S. Coast Guard to carry up to 1,000 passengers in a theme park.

She had twin screws with eight engines, four mounted on each propeller shaft. She also had two generators, and all these were located in a small, dark engine room. Running along each shaft was a thin steel rod that was used to reverse the propellers for slowing or stopping.

I'm not an engineer, nor am I entirely serious when I say I thought it was perfect. But being the thorough person I pretended to be, I asked John Roper to fly out some of his people from Norfolk Shipbuilding to look it over and send me a report. The report came back generally favorable. It said the Detroit engines were similar to very big bus engines and could be maintained with paper clips and rubber bands. Obviously this was blatant exaggeration for effect.

The next step was to have her inspected by the Coast Guard before putting her back into service. I accompanied the commander in charge of the Detroit office during his inspection. She passed, and we purchased her without financing. I later wished he had been a little more meticulous. She needed a fair amount of maintenance and cleanup, which we scheduled to have done in a Detroit shipyard. It was then late April and we planned to take her to Norfolk for some major shipyard repairs and installation of a full galley, with the start of full operations in early summer.

We hired a captain and sent him to Detroit to supervise the yard work. Now the fun began. The repair work was more than a month behind schedule, and new and costly jobs were added constantly. Finally, we were ready to go. We sent a delivery crew of four from Norfolk to join the vessel.

The captain was the first of four needed to complete this incredible voyage. One was reported to have shouted "Which way to Buffalo?" at a passing ship in the Great Lakes. He was released, and we managed to find three more equally incompetent captains. They seemed to keep getting sick and leaving at various points along the way. We finally discovered the underlying reason: the reversible-pitch propellers were unreliable, and thus the ship had trouble stopping.

Our little company was in a state of fear and despair. We began a procedure of having our executive staff convene near the end of the day, at four o'clock, to get a report. It was usually quite glum.

The ship continued on, and one rainy night in the Strait of Canso it entered a lock that lowers the ships to a different level. There's a strong steel restraining wire to protect the lock. Apparently the ship went careening into the lock and hit the restraining wire. She also sank the crane that lifted the wire. The captain called me at about seven in the evening and reported the day's events. He mentioned that both propellers were hanging down and the ship was holding up a number of big ships in the St. Lawrence Seaway. He asked what he should do.

We decided he should hire a tugboat and tow the ship to the nearest shipyard. The next morning he informed me that American tugboats were on strike. We ended up hiring a tugboat from Nova Scotia to haul our ship to Halifax. Work on the engines and propellers was finally finished in about three weeks. Again we were ready to proceed to Norfolk. Then I got word that the dry dock was not working properly, and we were marooned for another week.

It was then that I told the crew I was going to fly to Nova Scotia and bring it back myself. I received a call a couple of hours later informing me that this was unacceptable. I had a lot of experience, I was told, but not on a small ship, especially one like this. They were absolutely correct.

About a week later, I got a call that she had arrived and was anchored off Cape Henry, Virginia. I immediately rushed to the shoreline. There was our great hope sitting out there looking like a smoking hulk. We made an executive decision not to bring her to her berth in downtown Norfolk, but instead to hide her at a pier in Portsmouth.

We mounted a major effort to get her painted, cleaned up, and to some extent decorated. We ordered new tables and chairs, but deferred the major installation of her galley until we took her to her berth in Norfolk.

The media were now calling our offices about where the ship was. But they never discovered that she was in Portsmouth. A week or so later we were ready to move her. We had engaged a new captain, who was a former Navy chief petty officer. Our ship was named the *Spirit of Norfolk*, and we set the date to move her to Norfolk, a distance of just a few miles. The dock, in the center of downtown Norfolk, was terrible. It was full of riprap (rocks) and other discarded junk, wood, and rats. The whole area was used for automobile parking in the daytime and no one went downtown at night. To an extent, we were trailblazing by trying

Barbara and Tom Mountjoy at work on the first Spirit of Norfolk.

to attract Virginia Beach tourists to a dark downtown waterfront. It has greatly improved since.

The plan was to dock her and then have the press and some special guests aboard for cocktails. We were actually going to take her to Norfolk the night before the event. I went to Portsmouth to check on preparations and found the captain drinking beer. I delayed the move until very early the next morning and asked him if he did that in the Navy.

The ship arrived in time but with a terrible docking, including breaking a water pipe. I had wanted it to be a smashing event, but not literally! In addition, the new personnel couldn't find the boxes of drinking glasses. We hurriedly purchased more. Everything was in such a state of chaos that I canceled the underway cocktail party and we held it at the dock. Not a good beginning.

The following weeks were filled with harassment by the Coast Guard, the Norfolk Health Department, and city officials. I remember the head of the health department telling me that if one rat got on the ship, he would shut us down. I replied that they were *his* rats. He also told us that all drinks sold on the second deck, which was open, had to be served through a screen. No open bars for the *Spirit of Norfolk*.

Somehow we got a full-scale galley constructed, but not without a lot of difficulty, including having to build what I think was called a Class A60 bulkhead. The only problem then was that we had not finally decided what we were going to serve for food. It ended up being coq au vin.

It was now well into September and most of the tourists had left! On our very first cruise the ship came back and crashed into the head of the dock in downtown Norfolk and my ex–Navy captain tragically died of a heart attack while giving the order to the first mate to get a line ashore; otherwise the ship's bow would have been permanently embedded in Waterside Drive.

Finally we began what was to be our normal schedule. That consisted of two three-hour cruises per day: a luncheon cruise and a dinner cruise with drinks and some live music. We offered sightseeing in one of the greatest harbors in the world. In addition, the crew performed a Broadway and patriotic revue. Rarely was a cruise uneventful, however.

I don't want to imply that we were always having trouble, but we certainly had more than our share. There were engine problems. We seldom had all eight engines running together. The problems with the reversible-pitch propellers continued. Our friend John Roper saved our skin on many occasions. He would get us into one of his dry docks ahead of large oceangoing ships to repair the reversible-pitch problems. He would lend us his tugboat, the *George Roper*, which would tie up alongside and take the *Spirit* on her scheduled cruise. At night, the passengers never knew anything unusual was happening.

During the fall, I would go to the pier and watch the luncheon disembarkation process. My main purpose was to get the passenger count, which was increasing. I erroneously thought we were beginning to make money, but soon found out that because of additional expenses, the break-even point was rising faster than the passenger count. We ended operations in November and made a decision to rebuild the diesel engines. We hired a former naval engineer and he worked on them all winter. After the first spring cruise, we knew he had done anything but a perfect job. In fact, we had a breakdown on the first cruise with John Roper on board.

We had an okay summer season with pretty good passenger counts. As we approached fall, we realized that because of the shortness of the season we would still lose a little money. Therefore, we decided to explore the idea of moving her to Miami for the winter and changing her name to the *Spirit of Miami*.

Barbara and I flew to Miami and talked to tourist officials and the mayor. We ended up negotiating a lease for a pier at Bicentennial Park, which is right off Biscayne Boulevard in downtown Miami. It's a beautiful park, but it had problems we didn't know about. We made the commitment to move some employees to Miami for the winter, including renting apartments for sales personnel.

I noticed before we left that the Norfolk Coast Guard was putting more-stringent and additional requirements on the vessel. We complied, and a little before departure time I learned that it was because of the commanding officer of the Coast Guard in Miami. It seems he was a very tough character with little regard for public opinion. He had just required a large passenger liner to cancel a cruise and fly home all of its passengers because of a safety violation. The incident was widely reported. Apparently the Norfolk Coast Guard was concerned that our vessel would cause them embarrassment.

Also, we realized that we would have to restencil the 1,000 life jackets to say *Spirit of Miami* instead of *Spirit of Norfolk*. In what I thought was a wise move, we hired a large van and took them to an open field. To save money, we hired three of our daughters and their friends to do the work. For a while it seemed to be working well. Soon, however, Megan, Stephanie, Danielle, and their friends got bored. They then proceeded to spray-paint the trailer with their names and some additional "design" work. I ended up having to repaint the whole trailer, so it was not much of a cost-saving move.

The ship set sail for Miami and for several days she sent only routine messages, which was refreshing. That didn't last long. I awoke one morning, turned on the television, and there was a picture of the *Spirit of Miami* impaled on the Jacksonville Bridge, tying up traffic for miles.

The ship somehow proceeded and finally arrived in Miami. The ship was immediately put under certain restrictions by the Coast Guard. She was not to leave the *cut*, a channel out to sea. We had to get a captain with a higher license and the ship would have to have a special Coast Guard inspection in a few weeks.

We began operations, and in the first three days the ship hit a buoy, had a mild grounding, and gently sideswiped a ship at a dock. We let this more experienced captain go. Tom Mountjoy wrote on a copy of his license "Capt. Magoo," after the semi-blind cartoon character. Fortunately, the captain of the ship we hit was a Kings Pointer, and he was very nice to us.

At about this time, a picture appeared on the front page of the *Miami Herald* of a dead man lying in a pool of blood. The background was the *Spirit of Miami*. The captain explained that Bicentennial Park, in addition to being beautiful, was a mecca for criminals.

The Coast Guard imposed more conditions on us. At the same time, the crew organized a union election with the Department of Labor. We eventually avoided a union by one vote.

The Coast Guard was another matter. I decided to see the feared commanding officer, whose name was Colichio. This name sounded familiar but I attributed that to newspaper reports. When I entered his office he said, "Have you ever sailed on the United States Lines ship *American Chief*?" It turns out that he had also worked for United States Lines and had served on that same ship. Relations with the Coast Guard greatly improved. This is not to say that he broke any rules for us, but this coincidence was like a light in an otherwise obscured atmosphere.

We then had to find a captain with a higher license. He turned out to be Swedish and could speak very little English. The next order of business was marketing. We scheduled a cruise for about 300 hotel concierges and other people who could direct business to us. We held it on a beautiful evening and I was aboard.

I allowed the captain to go just outside the cut so there would be a view of the hotels along Miami Beach. Everything was peaceful and lovely. I was on the bridge with the captain when much to my dismay the engines started shutting down, one at a time, all eight of them. The emergency generators came on and although we couldn't move, the party roared on down below. There was a band playing and plenty of libations. We hired a tug and made our way back to the dock. I doubt if more than a few revelers knew there was anything out of the ordinary.

At that time, many South Americans were coming to Miami to shop, so the thrust of our marketing was to capture the Latino market. We tried hiring a Latino band and changing the food to what we thought was to their taste, but we never had any real success.

We got into some form of a normal operation and soldiered on. We even sponsored a Christmas dinner party at the dock for our business partner, Carnival Cruise Lines. Bob Dickinson asks to this day what kind of mystery rubber fish we served!

By the middle of the season, it had become clear that the Norfolk/Miami operation would not be profitable and that our other profit centers were subsidizing it. I remember a day back in Norfolk when Jim Denton said to me, "This is eating us alive. We have to get rid of it." I agreed.

I basically closed my office door and turned my attention full-time to finding a buyer. I placed ads in all the newspapers, including the *Wall Street Journal*, and in large metropolitan areas. I received all sorts of crazy offers, including land and restaurant swaps. Finally, we got what seemed like a serious offer. An executive from Pittsburgh wanted to fly to Miami in his private jet to see the ship. He owned ships. I caught a flight the same day. The next day he was supposed to be in our office at Bicentennial Park at three o'clock. At five-fifteen he still wasn't there, nor had he called. When the phone finally rang, I had disciplined myself not to answer on the first ring, but rather to wait for three.

He finally arrived with an entourage of five or six. We all went to dinner and made plans for a sea trial the next day. I learned at dinner that he was quite fond of an expensive white wine. I made sure we had a good supply on board. We left the dock, entourage included, and sailed out to the end of the cut. I was more than a little nervous and was especially concerned about the forthcoming docking. I made certain we were all inside drinking the white wine when it occurred. The docking turned out to be perfect. What happened next was the kind of gamesmanship that only two Irish businessmen can pull off, and it took a couple of months to consummate the deal.

Along the way he told me that I simply didn't know how to operate a ship. I humbly agreed, and it was his.

She first went to Pittsburgh and then to New York. I know she was still operating in New York in 2001. I was at the Lobster Festival in Rockland, Maine, and saw a remarkable photograph of the World Trade Center taken five days before 9/11. In the lower-right corner I was more than surprised to see the former *Spirit of Norfolk/Miami* chugging along at the ripe old age of sixty. I had several huge pictures made for my home and office. It was the end of one hell of an experience and I was sure I was through with the harbor-cruise business.

I was recently looking through the minutes of the board of director's meeting for January 31, 1980. The following excerpt comes from the middle of a lot of board business: "Following this, the Chairman reported in considerable detail the continuing source of difficulty with the operation of the *Spirit*, citing Coast Guard inspections and requirements, mechanical breakdowns, crew personnel reliability, and the current effort of a local union to organize the crew of the vessel." It all sounds straightforward and simple. It wasn't.

19

Interlude

e turned our attention to the other operations of our company, which thankfully were doing well. We were filling cruise ships to nice levels. The travel business was expanding with a number of new offices.

Mr. Happy raised his head again at the time of negotiations with Carnival Cruise Lines, and this time he almost had it cut off. He called a local TV station and told the people there that we were going bankrupt and that I had gone back to my investors a number of times. On this occasion the station recorded him, and he had to apologize for making false statements. He was soon gone from the scene. For the record, I never went back to my investors for additional funds. We didn't even use the notes they originally signed. A good number of them invested in subsequent offerings and in the establishment of a travel company in Naples, Florida. There were a few comments at board meetings about the experience with the *Spirit of Norfolk/Miami* being good research and development, but they didn't come from me.

There was some change in the company's stock structure. Some stock was bought so I now owned more than fifty percent of the company and had control. My share of ownership eventually went to about seventy percent. I never used the title "chairman" until the company was more than thirty years old. This was in deference to the seniority and experience of the other board members.

Sometime in the early eighties it became necessary for Barbara to have a hysterectomy. This was a traumatic event for her, and perhaps even more so for me. I took her to the hospital early in the morning and spent the next few hours in its chapel. The operation was routine and she was fine except that she discovered that she was allergic to morphine. I went to bed that evening very tired and much relieved.

The phone rang at about midnight and I immediately thought it was the hospital. It wasn't; it was Captain Gregory Avedelous, the master of the Celebrity Cruise ship *Meridian*. Captain Avedelous was an old friend from Greek Line days, and we had been marketing the *Meridian* for a number of years.

The ship was at anchor in Hampton Roads (Norfolk Harbor). I learned that there had been an accident off Miami that involved getting a large mooring line caught in one of the propellers. The ship had limped up to Virginia on one engine. John Chandris, another old friend and the owner of the ship, was on board. He wanted me to call John Roper and see if Norfolk Shipbuilding could dry-dock the ship in the morning. I made the midnight call and found that Norfolk Shipbuilding couldn't find a dry-dock space for nearly a month. I reported the bad news and went back to sleep.

The next morning my secretary forwarded a call to me in the hospital from John Chandris. He asked me if I would call the president of Newport News Shipbuilding and Drydock Company and use my influence to get him a meeting.

I knew the president of the shipyard but not well. In fact, we took care of the shipyard's commercial travel. I had recently received a copy of our newsletter, *The Traveler*, back from him after he had corrected, in red, the misspelling of the name of the mayor of Newport News and a couple of other errors. Also, I knew that Newport News Shipbuilding was involved primarily in the construction of U.S. Navy aircraft carriers and submarines, so I was not hopeful. The only good thing I could think of was that I had made a small donation to some young people's organization at his request.

I called the president's secretary, and asked if he would see Mr. Chandris, who had an emergency situation. She called me back and said the answer was yes, and gave me the time, which was one o'clock that same day.

I was relieved, and thought I was out of the situation. I passed this on to the captain, who passed it on to Mr. Chandris. The phone in the hospital rang for me again about a half hour later and it was the captain, this time telling me that Mr. Chandris would greatly appreciate it if I would accompany him to the meeting. I was flustered and told him about Barbara's operation and adverse morphine reaction, and that it would be very difficult for me to do.

I talked to Barbara about it. Despite the fact that it would show that I hardly knew the president and had little or no influence, she convinced me to go. I called the captain and said I'd be there.

At the shipyard, I sat in a downstairs waiting room with the captain and Mr. Chandris expecting the worst. At the appointed time, the door opened and the president of the shipyard and one of his assistants came down the stairs. They led us up to his office.

To my amazement, the president started with something like this: "We're very busy and do mostly military work, but when Richard O'Leary calls in this town, we go all out to see if we can help." To my astonishment he went on to make arrangements to move a submarine out of the dry dock the next day to make the necessary repairs while the captain, Mr. Chandris, and I were sitting there. I couldn't believe what had just transpired.

It was late afternoon before I got back to the hospital. When I entered Barbara's room, there were three dozen red roses with a card signed "John." I first thought that my wife had a secret lover. The next morning John Chandris called me and told me that he wanted to have a gala reception dinner on the ship for all the employees of Cruise International before she left the next morning for dry dock.

I later learned the long delay that was first contemplated would have amounted to more than 6 million dollars in lost revenue. John Chandris has said to me a number of times that "a man who would leave his sick wife to help a friend is a friend indeed, and a friend for life." Have you ever heard of the luck of the Irish?

At about this time, we established a profit-sharing plan that donated fifteen percent to our employees. This was highly motivational.

We continued our major air-package programs to Las Vegas, Epcot at Disney World, and Mexico, and sold chartered planes to Europe from Norfolk. We moved the Virginia Realtors and the Virginia Bar to Bermuda by air. Our commercial business continued to grow and we were opening operations away from Norfolk.

We announced plans for a new beautiful waterfront office headquarters. It won an award for architecture. We also greatly enlarged our in-house advertising department.

The city of Norfolk announced the construction of a major development on the downtown waterfront, a James Rouse project. Barbara and I love Boston and were familiar with the exciting Rouse project at Faneuil Hall. The proposed project had restaurants and shops right on the harbor. It also called for a dock, which, it was assumed, would be used by the boat *Carrie B*.

This announcement caught the attention of our staff. We wondered how we could participate. Although we considered a number of alternatives, the same answer kept coming up—we needed a ship.

The logic espoused by a number of staff members was that with our previous venture we had had the right concept but the wrong ship. I ran it by our board and we decided to build a ship. There were a number of obstacles to overcome, including obtaining the financing, selecting a shipyard, getting a State Corporation Commission Department license, and signing a dock lease. None of these was simple. These were the major items, but there were hundreds of others.

We decided to form a limited liability corporation, which requires an enormous amount of legal work and the preparation of an offering memorandum.

The State Corporation Commission license turned out to be a huge problem. The owners of the *Carrie B*, a Portsmouth company, opposed our application because they said it would hurt their business. They hired the state attorney general, who was also in private practice. It was a major hearing fully covered by the press. It took place in the state capital, Richmond. We hired a noted attorney who also was in the legislature. Our argument was that more advertising and promotion meant more business for everyone. We prevailed, and we were correct. They eventually cut their boat in half and added a middle section, in order to lengthen it.

Although the city wanted us to build a ship and use the new dock, that wasn't simple either. Our total investment would be in the millions of dollars, and we took the position that we wouldn't go forward unless we had exclusive use of the dock. The *Carrie B* owners raised hell, but at a raucous city hall meeting we prevailed again. The *Carrie B* continued to operate at the dock she had been using.

Bear with me as I interrupt my tale of how we got our first new ship built and in operation. I just described the Norfolk City Hall meeting as raucous. It really wasn't even that. Jim Denton, a former colleague, still a close friend, and now publisher of *World Affairs*, wrote a somewhat different version of this event for the book of memories that was presented to me at my retirement dinner. He loves to read it to people, and so I present the whole thing here for your enjoyment. Then I'll pick up where I left off.

A Memo for the Record, from Jim Denton

In a recent flash of self-deprecation, Richard asked me to write a scaled-back version of a tale that, at the slightest urging, I tell about the time he addressed the Norfolk City Council in the early 1980s to tidy up matters (read: stack the deck) so he could build and launch the new Spirit of Norfolk—*the vessel destined to be the lead ship in a fleet that would soon sail and flourish in harbors across America. He said he might include the story in his memoir.*

What Richard didn't mention, perhaps, was the story might ease his guilt because it offered the reader an elusive glimpse into an element of his nature that otherwise might not shine through in his own recounting of his life's journey.

I submit this offering, therefore, both to give insight and to pay tribute to Richard's "charm" and his quintessential American story. I do so with your indulgence, knowing that a detail here or there might be misplaced or exaggerated. But to those who know Richard Himself, the basic story will ring ever so true.

After years of mind-numbing studies, the visionaries of Norfolk's city council approved a James Rouse Company development project dubbed Waterside—a cluster of restaurants and shops and parks that promised to breathe new life into the city's abandoned and dilapidated downtown waterfront. Not surprisingly, Richard had a vision as well that involved building a ship to complement the city's revitalization efforts and, along the way, revolutionize the tired harbor tour industry across America.

With his vision in mind, Richard went about stacking the deck—I mean putting a deal together—that included a proposal that the city provide a few token gestures of goodwill or, more candidly—and it's difficult to put this delicately—incentives that amounted to preferential treatment. Actually, he was looking for Very Preferential Treatment. You see, Richard Himself reasoned that since he was taking a hell of a lot of OPM (Other People's Money) to build his ship, why shouldn't the city build, say, a new pier to protect and showcase his investment? And why not grant exclusive use of that pier, the parking lot, and the services—all at no cost? And, for that matter, shouldn't the city throw in free fuel and, sure, champagne and dancing girls—all compliments of the grateful taxpayers? Oh, did I mention the tax breaks, the bond deal, and His demand that all forms of tour-boat competition be banished to an untidy swamp twenty miles upriver?

Upon learning of His proposal, some council members and citizens, particularly those poor devils preparing to paddle through the stench upriver, thought perhaps Richard Himself's deal a trifle excessive. "Dancing Girls Too!" the headlines screamed.

Nonetheless, in the following weeks, His proposal tiptoed and slithered through the city's approval process until, at last, the planning commission approved His terms at one of those awkward three-in-the-morning meetings that huddled in a dark alley on about twenty minutes' notice. Thus, with more than a hint of controversy in the air, the stage was set for the city council's public session when the final vote would be cast to seal the fate of His proposal.

Arriving at the meeting one chilly Tuesday evening, I and my comrades on Richard's staff took two front-row seats that offered a full view of the spectacle about to unfold. Himself, poised for the Mother of All Battles, arrived armed with a stirring forty-minute speech calculated to comfortably fit his ten minutes of allotted time. His rhetoric would soar into an unrelenting defense of entrepreneurial capitalism and public-private "partnerships" with stern admonitions for anyone daring to impede their progress.

The proceedings began with the usual string of humble and nervous citizens, timidly approaching the city fathers to bid for a permit here or a license there. A neighbor's tree hung over a property line. Some children asked the city to build a park. All the while, the city manager offered the fine citizens helpful hints on council-meeting decorum. "Now friends, watch the little panel of lights. When the yellow light comes on, that means you have two minutes remaining to finish your remarks. And if you're still speaking when the red light turns on, a buzzer will sound to let everyone know it's time for another good Norfolkian to speak," he said. "We want to give all the good citizens their fair share of time to address the council," observed this champion of transparency, fairness, and the American way. In all, 'twas a tidy affair that would have moistened the eyes of Norman Rockwell.

And then Richard was called forward, and his formal introduction began.

As Richard positioned Himself before the microphone—muscles strained and wound tight before the enemy—the most unexpected thing was happening. The mayor was smiling deferentially and was introducing Himself to the assembled as "a visionary son of Norfolk." These were not the words of a hostile council. The mayor continued, "Himself is the very personification of America's entrepreneurial spirit." Baroque, now even embarrassing in his praise, the mayor welcomed "this son of an immigrant Irish dockworker who had fought his way through the school of hard knocks, the youngest officer to serve on the decks of the SS *United States*, the youngest commandant of the Merchant Marine Academy at

Kings Point." His voice rising, the mayor was relentless, and then he said, "It was Richard Himself who came to Norfolk some years ago to deliver us from our ignorance and champion revolutionary development of our city's harbor, making it a world-class port, bringing cruise ships to our docks, glory to our city, and gold to our treasury."

Thoughtfully leaving out the OPM part, the mayor concluded with something like this: "Clearly, Himself's proposal for Excessive Preferential Treatment is reasonable, given His leadership and the risks he is about to take at Waterside." Booming now, he said, "You want incentives, Richard? Yes, take them all, Richard! Everything! It's yours!"

As the mayor's words trailed off, a respectful hush fell over the assembled citizenry. My jaw sagging, I looked up in disbelief, expecting the roof to part and witness angels drifting down, with trumpets blowing sweetly to herald Richard's triumph, as a conqueror's wreath was laid gently on His fair head. This is beauty itself, I thought. Too good to be true. Himself won without firing a shot. Not even raising his musket.

But Richard would have no part of this charade! He had brought His bazooka and nothing—surely not a mere unconditional surrender—was going to stop Him from blasting away! As a Goliath looms before hapless Davids, there Himself stood—tone deaf and dangerously alone before the microphone—poised to snatch defeat from the jaws of victory.

His response to the mayor's naked and unapologetic adulation began with something like this: "Okay, you bastards, first you can turn off those dainty lights and that stupid buzzer because I'm here to say what's on my mind. And you can forget those time limits." And thus Himself launched into His presentation (read: diatribe), which would have been brilliant had he had an enemy other than Himself within earshot.

We on the staff slumped, stunned into stupor, as flashes of yellow and red streaked across the ceiling where angels had lingered just moments before. Himself lectured and admonished on—now crashing through a room consumed by wailing sirens and screaming buzzers.

For their part, the council members were showing all the signs of traumatic shock: eyes glazed and rolling back, heads tilted limply to one side or the other, lips moving soundlessly. Poor souls. Their disorientation was so complete that when it came time to vote, they simply stared forward and blankly and numbly mumbled, "Pleeeease, give that man anything he wants. Anything . . ."

In their defense, the council members were stunned, at least for the moment, beyond the outer limits of their capacity to comprehend just what exactly had happened. We could only thank Heaven for the faint of heart among us and that they dominated the council that night.

Epilogue

Reading back now, I'm not so sure it went exactly how I've described it. But let me say that Richard was welcomed by the good council members with unanticipated generosity and Richard was less impressed than the rest of us. And yes, he did have something on his mind. And yes, he did tell the council that it could dispense with those time limits, though perhaps in more modest terms.

But Richard won, as he usually has, does, and will. The city, I should add, did exceptionally well by those incentives—as did those who had the foresight to hand over OPM. And yes, Richard did all right too. And, from my perspective, anyway, he wins because he's smart, determined, fair, and generous. And we thank him because he has inspired and guided so many lives more than he can possibly know. And for that, we are all better, richer in spirit, making us all the more in his debt.

He and his Barbara are admired and loved friends and teachers to whom I and my family owe so much.

Now back to building the first new *Spirit* vessel. Raising the money was the easiest part. We called together a group of about sixty, some of them our original investors. We passed out the offering memorandum with all the required legalese telling them why they shouldn't invest. We easily sold the thirty packages, and it would get easier in the future.

We put out a request for proposal to three shipyards. I went to Warren, Rhode Island, and met with Luther Blount, the owner of Blount Boats. There was little doubt who would get the award; Luther Blount was a real character.

Little did I know that we would build eleven ships with him over the course of a decade. He was cantankerous, experienced, and brilliant. I always told him he was the only business owner I had ever met whose philosophy was that the customer is always wrong.

He was an inventor who held dozens of patents. I got to know him very well and loved every moment of our time together. We

The Spirit of Norfolk *under construction at Blount Boats.*

traveled some with him, and Barbara and I once dined at one of his houses, on Prudence Island, which is in the middle of Narragansett Bay. He had a raised hunting station, a shotgun that he made himself, and a bow and arrow, also made by him. When we were there, he was trying to grow artificial oysters. That night we had a dinner of venison he had shot and vegetables he had grown or taken from the root cellar. He also made the wine from elderberries. Not so good on the wine.

Signing a contract with Luther Blount as Tom Mountjoy looks on.

He was proud of the fact that he had built a hundred small ships. He had pictures in his office of every one of them. I told him that one was more ugly than the next until I came along. We did build better and better boats together. They really got better looking and they got bigger. About ten months after the contract was signed, my Barbara christened our *Spirit of Norfolk*, and we were ready to leave for Virginia.

Barbara christening the new Spirit of Norfolk.

Our motley crew: C.I. staff, Spirit *staff, friends, and our daughter Danielle.*

This time I took our new vessel to Virginia myself, with a stop in New York City for the hell of it. The crew was made up of people from the company and some friends and family. The whole, rather motley, crew of twenty ended up at P. J. Clarke's, the famous East Side bar. To say we had a good time doesn't do justice to the story. In the middle of the nonsense, Kitty Carlisle, the famous singer, actress, and TV personality, complained to Barbara, "If you want to do this, hire a hall." The boisterousness decreased for about seven minutes.

It was a beautiful, successful trip. We arrived off Cape Henry at about six in the morning. Coming up the channel, Barbara was steering. I had gone below to get coffee and was on my way back to the bridge when I saw a huge submarine surfacing right behind us. I went quietly up to Barbara and said, "Don't look now, but . . ."

A press helicopter followed us in. We arrived at the dock at about nine. We had come a long way since the original *Spirit*. Everything was new. We had two live bands and the crew performed a Broadway and patriotic revue. The food, with three entrées, was served in buffet lines on two decks. And, of course, we had several good bars.

We already knew by the advance bookings that we had a huge success on our hands. This was thirty years ago, and I believe the *Spirit* is the only surviving original business at Waterside. We were off and running, as the saying goes, and we began to think about which port we would go to next.

Boarding the Spirit of Norfolk *for the company Christmas party.*

20

The Launching of the *Spirit*s

Spirit of Philadelphia

When we first considered Philadelphia, I was skeptical. The city didn't have an attractive waterfront. The Delaware River is a commercial waterway and not a place for nice-looking boats.

We went through the usual procedures, but no license was necessary. The same limited liability and offering memorandums applied, though. This was, however, a much easier sell to investors.

I again went to Rhode Island and again delivered the vessel, but we ran into very rough weather before we got to the mouth of the Delaware. I turned her into Atlantic City and put her on the Coast Guard dock without permission. There was no other choice. This delayed us twenty-four hours, so we reached the dock in Philadelphia with one day to load—among other things—tables, chairs, dishes, and food for 600 people. As I left the ship, I saw some highly spirited young people running around. They basically worked through the night, and the next day we sailed on time for the inaugural cruise.

The Spirit of Philadelphia.

Once again, we knew we had a big hit by the advance bookings. In fact, the *Spirit of Philadelphia* was for many years our most popular ship. We think the fact that the city didn't have much of a waterfront actually increased the popularity of the ship.

Spirit of Washington

In Washington, D.C., there was a company with a couple of small boats. It seemed like a natural for our type of operation, and it was. We built a ship and made a business deal to lay up the small boats. (Sometime later we acquired a smaller vessel and called it the *Spirit of Mount Vernon*, and it was another success.)

My daughter Leslie became the sales manager and one of her charges was her younger sister Megan, who went on to become the leading group sales manager in the country. Megan was wonderful at selling groups on the idea of cruising on the *Spirit of Washington* because she instinctively understood two important principles. The first was how to close the deal. She received inquiries because of advertising, cold calling, and referrals, and she was tenacious about turning that mild interest into a sale without overpromising.

The second was delivering a product that fulfills or exceeds a customer's expectations. It's this second principle that this next vignette is based on. I used to love when she related this rather complicated story, which was really funny when she told it, rich with detail that made it hilarious. I can't replicate that detail, but I'll attempt to get across the idea of what happened.

Megan received a phone call from a woman who wanted to put on a gala bar mitzvah for her son. She seized on this and fed the client's interest with descriptions of what a glorious event this would be on the *Spirit of Washington*. This mother was detail oriented and already knew what she wanted, but Megan brought her to a new level of expectation. It seemed that money was no object, which makes for a wonderful situation for an accomplished salesperson.

This was to be a very large affair—no problem for the ship, as it could easily accommodate 600. Although the ship had two bands, a special band was engaged for the children, who would be on the first deck. The majority of the adults would be on the upper decks.

This woman was involved in everything, even the tiniest detail. She visited the ship numerous times during the planning period. The regular menu items were eliminated and she ordered exotic foods that were difficult to obtain. One of the features, maybe the key feature of the entire evening, was some very special pizza for the young people. It was from a famous pizza place in Washington, D.C. It was to be prepared and delivered to the ship thirty minutes before sailing time. Megan and the rest of the company staff were on board all afternoon, attending to the extensive checklist the woman had prepared.

An hour before sailing, the guests began arriving. Everything went routinely. Of course, Megan was a nervous wreck, as the woman followed her around and questioned everything. The ship sailed at exactly seven o'clock with the bands playing and the waiters and waitresses singing "Anchors Aweigh."

They were a short distance down the Potomac River when someone from the galley asked where the famous pizza was. Nobody knew! Megan and a host of others called the office, which was located on the pier. Nobody knew where the pizza was but somebody reported that he'd seen a truck from the pizza company. The *Spirit of Washington* was in panic mode. The decision was made: return to the pier and try to find an emergency load of that special pizza.

So far the hostess was unaware that anything was wrong. As the ship headed back, there were many people on phones to the office and to the pier. Finally a call came in from the office with the following message: The pizza had been left on the dock in large white plastic bags. A dockhand had seen the bags and, thinking they were trash, had thrown them into a large Dumpster. Preparations were underway to have dockhands climb into the Dumpster and try to retrieve the featured delicacy of the evening without anyone being the wiser.

Megan was busy distracting the hostess and making up reasons for the surprise docking. Miraculously, the ship and dock personnel got the carefully bagged, protected pizza on board without arousing attention, so the delay was only about twenty minutes. The bar mitzvah was a howling success. We even used a testimonial from the hostess in some of our group advertising. There has to be a moral here somewhere. Perhaps it's that careful attention to every detail but one can lead to a very bad outcome—unless you're very lucky. Fortunately, we were lucky and escaped what could have been a disaster.

While I'm writing about our daughters, I'd like to mention that in the early days of the *Spirit* ship operations, all seven of them, from time to time, worked as waitresses. The only problem with this is that waiters and waitresses on the *Spirit*s had to be able to sing and dance, as they were part of the Broadway revues performed on two decks to live music.

None of our daughters was a singer or a dancer except possibly Dione. They were all good actors, though. When necessity called, each joined the line and faked the singing and dancing routines—and got away with it.

Our daughter Danielle has many talents but singing and dancing are not among them. She has gone on to become a highly successful president of a large international fabric company that she co-founded.

However, a good number of years ago she was a waitress on the *Spirit of New York* while she was studying at Adelphi University. The ship, at the time, was docked at the foot of Wall Street in the East River.

This was during the go-go 1980s and lots of Wall Street types with their pockets stuffed with 100-dollar-bills frequented the ship. I was surprised to learn just recently that she would average 300 dollars in tips for a dinner cruise, and when she did the lunch, dinner, and midnight cruises she would average 1,000 dollars.

Many of the waiters and waitresses had actual Broadway experience and the shows on this ship were particularly good.

Danielle did not participate except in case of a real emergency, when she would join the line but no sound would come out of her mouth and her lack of dancing ability was probably noticed by some, but she was a great waitress. Normally, when the show, which lasted about twenty minutes, began on the deck she was working on, she would simply disappear to the galley or another deck.

I have always loved the story about a young Wall Street type who was obviously attracted to her. The first time she met him, he asked her when she was going to perform. She told him that she had just finished on the upper deck. He was a lavish tipper and she also enjoyed his company. He was back a couple of days later and he sat on the upper deck hoping to see her there. When he finally found her she was serving on the lower deck and explained to him that he had missed her again. I think he tried for a third time with a similar outcome and basically gave up.

She was actually quite attracted to him also, but sometimes things are just not meant to be.

Spirit of Boston

Our first worry in Boston was that because of the colder weather, we would have to shorten our season. This never turned out to be the case, as we learned how to market the ship right up until New Year's, primarily by marketing Christmas and New Year's Eve parties.

Then trouble again. Right at the start, Barbara and I went to see the mayor, who encouraged us. The International Longshoremen's Association (ILA), however, insisted that we hire four longshoremen to handle our lines and the gangway and to count passengers. Our operation couldn't support the kind of wages they demanded. I also knew that the practice would spread to other cities and then we'd be finished.

The city arranged for us to house our employees in a waterfront building. No one told us, though, that they had just evicted the ILA. One of our people saw a metal sign mounted on a rock near the front door, so we never moved in. We found some offices on the waterfront. The only problem here was that there was a

The Spirit of Boston.

large wholesale fish market downstairs and our personnel had to bring a change of clothing because of the smell.

The ship was completed and I brought it from Rhode Island to Boston, with the same type of crew but with different people. It arrived safely, but the next day we found half of our lines had been untied and the gangway was on the dock. I immediately asked for a meeting with the ILA leadership on the dock. What started with two people turned into a mob scene with about a hundred all around me. The associate I had with me retired behind a barrier.

I tried to tell them that we couldn't afford to hire them. They knew my name was a lot like theirs—that is, beginning with an O. There was a little light pushing and they said my father, who had been a Boston longshoreman, would be ashamed of me. I said he would not. I also told them that I thought the organization most to blame was the port authority. When this was over, I said, sometime in the future I'd take them to a bar and buy them some wine. That was stupid, and what seemed like a unanimous cry went up: "We don't drink wine!"

That was just the beginning. They left and put up a big picket line. Our inaugural sailing was the next day. The mayor and all the other official guests canceled.

We had trouble at first with the picket line. Not many people who had paid for their tickets would honor the line, but we had a hard time getting supplies and food, especially refrigerated food, into the area. We hired nonunion drivers and used a number of gateways, and kept changing them. We also hired off-duty state troopers as guards.

There was one major event that occurred. Governor Michael Dukakis was running for president at the time. His wife, Kitty, had asked us to donate the ship for a fund-raiser for the poor. We said yes. On the afternoon of the cruise, the governor's office called me and asked if I would call the owner of Anthony's Pier 4 Restaurant, a famous Boston institution located, as the name implies, on a pier in Boston Harbor. They wanted me to ask if we could move the ship there. They were obviously trying to find a way not to cross the picket line. I said I would, but I'd have to tell the union. I called Anthony Athanas, and he was less than polite. "You tell the governor that if he wants to make a request," he said, "he should do it himself, not send someone like you." By sailing time that evening, it was raining really hard but Governor Dukakis and Kitty crossed the picket line, and he was photographed doing so.

We put up with the picket line for the whole season. Gradually it dropped from eight or ten pickets to one, but it stayed. We then moved to a non-ILA pier.

New York Harbor

On July 4, 1986, the country held a birthday celebration in New York City that included the unveiling of the newly restored Statue of Liberty, which had been undergoing repairs for five years. It turned out to be a huge event and party. On Ellis Island, President Reagan was the featured speaker. The conclusion was an exciting display of fireworks. Interest was incredible. A round bar seat in a restaurant or bar along the waterfront sold for 1,000 dollars. Boats were in demand and we had an opportunity to charter the four *Spirit*s we owned at the time to large national organizations. My staff was once again a bit dubious about New York and the problems we might encounter. I was more interested in the profit potential we would encounter.

The *Spirit of Norfolk*, the *Spirit of Washington*, the *Spirit of Philadelphia*, and the *Spirit of Boston* were placed under charter. They sailed to New York and were all berthed on the old United States Lines pier at the foot of Thirty-fourth Street. (No longer in use, this is the same pier from which I sailed to Europe and the Far East.)

I also sailed my personal sailboat, a fifty-foot Hinckley, to New York for the weekend. On board we had our youngest daughter, Dione, and a young man named Baylor, who was working on the boat for the summer. Also on board was Barbara and Lindy, our poodle. The following account of some of the adventures

The Derryvahalla II.

of that weekend is written from the perspective of someone who lived in the New York area for sixteen years.

I know New York Harbor and its rivers almost as well as I know my own living room. This is because of the hundreds of sailings on a Navy ship, Merchant Marine freighters, the SS *United States*, and my dozen personal boats. I love the harbor and it never fails to thrill me.

By the way, this particular Hinckley was named the *Derryvahalla*. When we arrived in the upper harbor, I wanted a photograph of our boat under full sail in front of the Statue of Liberty. I lowered our ten-foot Dyer dinghy with Dione and a camera aboard, not without some protestations from Barbara. We left this very game young lady with a life jacket in the middle of the traffic of New York Harbor in a small fiberglass dinghy. This was perhaps not the most prudent thing I've ever done on the water, but Dione enjoyed it and we have a smashing picture of us in front of the Statue of Liberty.

We also brought our other daughters to New York. They slept on our boat and at various places on the four *Spirits*. To put it mildly, it was a great weekend. We took out my overloaded sailboat for an afternoon cruise. Dione put on a rubber Statue of Liberty crown and a sheet. As we approached a number of packed grandstands she waved, and a huge wave of cheers went up. New Yorkers were in a grand mood.

That night the *Spirits* and my sailboat were loaded with passengers. One of the *Spirits* had an enormous lipstick mounted on its top deck, courtesy of Revlon, the charterer.

A great flotilla left the docks on an absolutely spectacular evening. We had at least twenty-five people, mostly young, on my sailboat, and I was the only one on my boat, or perhaps on any other boat, who had not had something to drink.

The fireworks were wonderful. My staff's worries about New Yorkers proved to be unfounded. The crowds ashore and afloat were on their best behavior, as I suspected they would be.

There were two Australian boys, guests of our daughters, standing near me at the wheel. Fireworks were exploding all over the harbor and rivers of New York. The Australians kept shouting, "It's a bit of blahst, isn't it?" Indeed it was. The New York papers were filled with stories praising the weekend and the crowds.

The next day we were preparing the sailboat to leave for Maine when we noticed a number of large trays containing some wonderful leftover salmon from one of the *Spirits*. Dione and Baylor loaded them aboard.

We had planned to take out the *Spirits* for a group picture down near the Battery. This is the Times Square of boating. Nobody follows the Nautical Rules of the Road. Boat wakes stir up the water so that it feels as if you're in a terrible storm. This is also where the Staten Island ferries dock, at the foot of the Battery. These ferries think they own this stretch of the harbor and actually force other traffic to change course, in clear violation of the Rules of the Road.

At about seven-thirty in the morning, we proceeded down the Hudson on the *Derryvahalla* with some of my fretful staff aboard. The four *Spirit*s followed us in a line. This is the picture on the cover of the book. Of course, we met a Staten Island ferry, which I'm sure intended to make us move. I was steering my sailboat and talking on the VHF radio to our ships; the conversation went something like this.

Dione as the Statue of Liberty.

I told them to stay in line and hold course. The replies came back: "Richard, we can't, he's not going to change course." Again I ordered them to hold course. Again the voices came back: "Richard, we can't do that." But they did, and the ferry moved. Again, we got a wonderful picture. I commissioned an artist to make a painting of this scene. The new and bigger *Spirit of New York* was under construction in Rhode Island at the time, so I said to the artist, "Paint her in anyway." That painting now hangs upstairs from where I'm sitting, in our Maine home. I've thought about putting a title under it, *Danger at Sea*.

We left immediately for our various destinations: the *Spirit*s to their respective ports—Norfolk, Washington, Philadelphia, and Boston—and the *Derryvahalla* headed north—with our cargo of salmon—stopping nights in various ports.

We were eating a lot of salmon, and our two young crewmembers were getting tired of it. One evening, anchored near Block Island, I asked for the last of that salmon. A little later Dione came running below and told me a seagull flew in and took it off the grill. This happened more than twenty years ago, and Dione hasn't eaten salmon since. And she still insists the seagull story is true.

The Spirit of New York *brochure.*

Spirit of New York

I wanted to take a look at New York. Not only did I want to consider it, but also I wanted to build a much larger ship to make a bigger splash in this huge port and market. I discussed it at our weekly executive committee meeting. Everyone was afraid of New York. Our executives worried about crime, unions, dock space, and costs. They made a lot of cogent arguments, but I like New York and had lived in the area for sixteen years. You might say I knew the waterfront.

Anyone who knows me will tell you I almost always seek consensus, but not this time. I didn't have a single supporter out of eight members, and that included my wife.

There was some competition in our business in New York but not much, and it did not provide the quality product we were offering. I argued for building the biggest and best dinner-cruise ship in the business.

Some wanted to try it with the same vessels we had been so successful with in other big cities. I countered that the vessel had to be special simply because this was New York. I flew off by myself and met with the New York Port Authority and other city officials and people who controlled the docks. I ended up securing a dock lease with a real tycoon who controlled a dock at the foot of Wall Street. I can't say I felt comfortable with this character, but I got what I wanted.

I then flew to Rhode Island to meet with Luther, and we designed the new class of *Spirit* vessel. At 225 feet, it was about 40 feet longer than its predecessors, and had three decks rather than two. There was basically a large opening in the third deck so that passengers could hear the music and see the Broadway revues. We still needed only two bands.

Luther liked the concept and we started construction. We later built two of these boats at one time in his little shipyard. We began sales and marketing operations in New York, but our offices were in New Jersey. The reading on early advance bookings was quite good.

We finished construction in about a year and headed for the Big Apple. Once again I took the ship down myself. It was becoming a ritual: I'd take the ship

Waiters and waitresses on the Spirit of New York.

from the shipyard to the dock, turn it over to the captain, and never touch it again. I loved it.

There were a few problems with our previously mentioned leaseholder, or dockmaster, as he viewed himself. For example, the water hookup he provided was with a long garden hose. When I complained, he asked what the matter with me was. Didn't I know New York water was the best in the world? I explained that although that might be true, it couldn't come through a garden hose. We got it corrected.

It was time for our inaugural cruise. Almost all our waiter and waitress singers came right from Broadway. We had spent about 35,000 dollars for previous inaugural luncheons; we spent more than 50,000 in New York. The ship, though considerably larger, still held 600 passengers, the same as the smaller ships. We had the U.S. Merchant Marine Academy trumpeters perform and New York City fireboats sprayed plumes of water. Alair Townsend, the deputy mayor, symbolically christened the ship. "We are fortunate to have such a beautiful new ship from which to view one of the world's greatest vistas," she said. "I have little doubt that this ship is going to be one of New York City's spectacular star attractions."

I concluded my remarks by saying, "We've been doing business in most other East Coast cities with both ocean-cruise vessels and our own harbor vessels and we do quite an audacious thing. For the last six years, we've had a New York Broadway revue on each of our vessels. You'll soon see that show and in it hear a song you've heard about New York. The lyrics say, 'If I can make it there, I'll make

Maritime Day in New York City.

it anywhere.' Well, I want you to know that we've reversed that process. We've made it everywhere else, and I'm here to tell you today that we're now coming to make it here in New York."

We sailed with seven presidents of cruise lines among the 600 guests for lunch. That night we sailed with a New York Chamber of Commerce charter. Among the other guests (pictured above) were James Gifford, executive vice president of the New York Chamber of Commerce; Alair Townsend, deputy mayor of New York; David Rockefeller, chairman of the New York Chamber of Commerce; oh, and I almost forgot, Barbara O'Leary.

The ship produced sales of more than 8 million dollars in its first year. In May 1988, the ship hosted the Maritime Day celebration of the Port of New York.

Spirit of Chicago

Financing became easier. With success comes a sort of tribute. We had reached the point where it was possible to raise millions of dollars in equity financing in about thirty minutes. We would call a meeting and pass out the offering memorandums, with all their language cautioning against the possible perils ahead. There was always a clause warning potential investors to take home the memorandum and discuss it with their financial advisers. At the end of our meetings, most of the guests would walk out, leaving their checks on the table.

The *Spirit of Chicago* was built, and we sent her to Chicago via the inland route. This was the first *Spirit* that I didn't deliver. The ostensible reason was that I was a deep-water sailor and didn't know the way. The truth was I could no longer be away from my office for that long.

The Spirit of Chicago.

The ship was assigned to the Navy Pier. The wife of Governor Thompson of Illinois christened the ship while he stood outside his limousine in the background in order not to detract from her moment.

Spirit of Los Angeles

This new ship, too, was built by Blount Boats, but this one had a long way to go. It took a certain amount of boldness and a great deal of planning to pull this off. The preparation for the sea voyage, which was via the Panama Canal, was extensive. All of her hull openings had to be boarded up with heavy lumber. The main deck was full of barrels of fuel, all interconnected by pipes. We hired a captain who specialized in sailing a relatively small vessel on long voyages.

After all the preparation, the ship had a rather uneventful voyage. When she arrived, however, things were different from what we had anticipated. First, and most importantly, the advance group bookings were not good. Second, after a few months of operation, we were sued over the issue of name infringement. There was a small commercial boat with the word "spirit" in its name. Although

The Spirit of Los Angeles.

we'd thoroughly checked out all such details with the port authority, it was still a serious issue.

Our attorney recommended hiring the leading expert on patent law, who practiced in Washington, D.C. He charged an incredible fee but I was assured our problems were over. We went to court and lost. We had to change the name of the vessel to the *Pride of Los Angeles* and redo our promotional materials. When I asked the important attorney what had happened, he replied that the judge was prejudiced.

Business stayed at an unacceptable level, and we attempted several major adjustments, including hiring a West Coast advertising agency. Many people asked me what was wrong. My answer was usually "I don't know."

We followed the same plan that had produced success in other ports. With a lot of time to ponder it, now I think I know what happened. Our dock was in San Pedro, just south of Los Angeles. This is the place where boats leave for Catalina Island and the big cruise ships leave for Mexico. The ship was within easy view of the Harbor Freeway, which goes to Long Beach. Our cruises sailed down to Long Beach to the site of the *Queen Mary*, which is now a hotel. The views from the cruise were of oil rigs that are unsightly. I believe this was the problem. I think people decided this probably wasn't a nice place to cruise. Actually, at night the commercial lights made it quite attractive. We struggled on but success eluded us.

Spirit of Seattle

For this ship, we made the same preparations for an even longer sea voyage. This trip, too, was uneventful. Business in Seattle was acceptable, but after a few months we ran into a similar name issue as the one that had plagued us in Los Angeles. This time we merely complied, and our ship became the *Spirit of Puget Sound*. Out west, there must be something in the water.

Replacement Vessels

In Louisiana we constructed a replacement vessel for the *Spirit of Norfolk*. It was a sleek and futuristic-looking vessel.

Our last vessel, which was again with Blount Boats, replaced the *Spirit of Boston*. It was a beautiful ship, and this time there were no union problems. We had a very successful inaugural ceremony on Rowes Wharf, right in the heart of Boston.

21

Halcyon Days

With the exception of Los Angeles, Cruise International, the *Spirits*, and C.I. Travel were booming. Our ocean-cruise business was doing well and we were sailing and marketing out of four East Coast ports. We were ensconced in our new waterfront office building in Norfolk. We had fifty-five offices in a dozen states, including Hawaii, and one in Washington, D.C. We had an in-house advertising agency doing more than 8 million dollars in business annually, and had some 2,500 employees. The trade publication *Business Travel News* named just our travel division the thirtieth-largest company out of more than 2,000 travel agencies.

Our national purchasing department for the *Spirits* bought huge quantities of whatever we required. For example, we purchased 500,000 pounds of fish at a time.

We had a national entertainment department. We employed thirty-eight bands, and each year created our own Broadway revues, which were presented, along with menu changes, at our annual winter managers' meeting. I think it's fair to say that we had a highly spirited group of employees.

Little Harbor 75.

Hinckley Sou'wester.

Little Harbor 75.

Hinckley picnic boat.

I called this section Halcyon Days because all areas of the company were doing well. Although there are always problems somewhere in an enterprise of this size, this was a period of relative calm which I could expand on. However, I have decided to include under this same heading a section on my personal boats. These boats gave my family, friends, and me much joy,

Pearson 424.

adventure, and happiness, and they complement the theme of this book.

Of all the personal boats I have owned, I have a favorite. It was not the biggest or the most expensive. It is the boat on the cover of this book. It was a fifty-foot Hinckley Sou'wester that I named *Derryvahalla*, after my father's townland in Ireland.

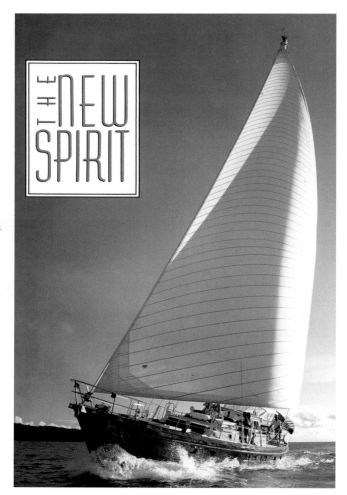

Right: 75' Little Harbor, New Spirit.

Below: 72' Viking Sport Cruiser, La Mia Barbéra.

Friends and family who shared our boating excursions over the years.

Hinckleys were known as the ultimate yacht in the world of sailing. It was more than buying a boat, it was like joining an exclusive club that very few people ever had the privilege to experience.

My Hinckley was my second sailboat. I traded in a Pearson 424 and I became the second owner of an incredible boat that was beautiful and functionally perfect.

The day I went to pick her up in Southwest Harbor, Maine, was one of the most exciting days of my life. Barbara and I flew into Bangor, Maine, with my youngest daughter, Megan. I was more than excited, I was ecstatic.

The ride from Bangor to Southwest Harbor, a distance of about fifty miles, seemed like an eternity. Finally we arrived and I looked at my freshly painted midnight green Hinckley with great joy. We left the same evening for an overnight cruise with Hank Halsted and I doubt if I had ever been happier.

I owned the boat for seven years and part of the experience was getting to know the people of the Hinckley Company. We went back every year for drydocking and came to appreciate the skilled Hinckley workers. We actually got to know many of them, including Bob Hinckley, the president, and his wife, Tina, as well as Shep McKenney, one of the owners who was from Maryland.

Years later, we obtained a third standard poodle. We soon realized that we could not stay in our beautiful eighteenth-floor apartment on the beach in Naples, Florida. It came down to letting the third poodle go or moving from our home of ten years. We chose to move.

We were fortunate to find a great home nearby on Venetian Bay. It had a ninety-foot dock and all kinds of other great features. Several days before we were scheduled to move in we went to a popular eating place called Cloyd's Steak and Lobster House. We were with longtime friends Maureen and Walter "Moe" Ray and Diane and Tom Ouverson. At the very next table was an attractive couple that I was conversing with.

It turned out that the charming lady was named Laurie and she is a Hinckley. She is in fact the niece of the famous Henry Hinckley, the son of the founder of the company. Of more importance, they live one house down from our new home. Her husband's name is Freddie Tower and he formerly worked in the high tech financial computer field. He had his own company and invented some very important financial computer programs that he sold to most big financial companies. He is also charming and an all-around fascinating character.

We also both own Hinckley picnic boats, which are docked behind our houses. Freddie is more than charming, he is a whirlwind of activity. He has had a strong influence on me, particularly in my social life. I was never one to do much socializing. In fact, I have mentioned more than once that I am working on becoming a recluse. Although I say this humorously, there is some truth to it. But thanks to Freddie, I am now a proud member of the Naples Yacht Club and a member of several social groups that I enjoy very much. It was certainly a fortuitous event for us to become neighbors with them.

The Hinckley boat story has a rather surprising ending. I had many happy cruises on her. I then sold her to the commodore of the Corinthian Yacht Club, an international sailing organization, and he sailed her to Bantry Bay, Ireland, which is very close to Derryvahalla, the birthplace of my father.

We owned twelve personal boats over the years, both sail and power. They had such names as *Derryvahalla*, *New Spirit,* and several named *La Mia Barbéra*. One of the best known was a seventy-five-foot sailboat that we had for ten years. It was a Little Harbor built by the famous yachtsman, Ted Hood. It was large and strongly built and had a hundred-foot mast and two engines. She was also very luxurious.

We planned to attempt to charter her for about ten to twelve weeks per year. We sailed her in the Caribbean and Maine. She had a crew of three when under charter. We started with a crew that consisted of an ex-professor along with a petite woman who was an incredible chef. We also had a third person who assisted with everything.

When we first put the boat in service the boat participated in a fall cook-off in Antigua for all charter boats. Most of the boats were European and were much larger with larger crews. However, we won the award for best food for our first three years. That helped us a great deal in attracting notable guests. A Mr. Blanc, owner of *Elle* magazine in Paris, chartered her in the Caribbean each January for a number of years.

Courtney Ross, the widow of Steve Ross, founder of Time Warner, and her secretary chartered her a number of times in the Caribbean and in Maine. Jack Kent Cooke, the former owner of the Washington Redskins and other notable media enterprises, chartered her out of Newport, Rhode Island.

So we pretty much achieved our goal of ten weeks of charter, which left plenty of time for our use. We employed it for some business entertaining. I think Bob and Jodi Dickinson were on about ten times. Bob is the former president of Carnival Cruise Lines. We sold the boat in 1990 to Robert Mosbacher, brother of the noted yachtsman Emil "Bus" Mosbacher, who won the America's Cup twice. Robert was President George H. W. Bush's secretary of commerce.

We then shifted to powerboats and owned some very fine ones, including a seventy-two-foot Viking Sports Cruiser named *La Mia Barbéra V*. This is a very lush yacht. She is now in Athens, Greece, after being purchased from me by a Greek shipowner.

We enjoyed a lot of boating and I found what is known as a steaming partner whom I loved to operate boats with. His name is Kip Reynolds. He owns South Port Marine in South Portland, Maine. Other than Barbara there is no one I more enjoy being on the water with. We have sailed up and down the East Coast for a number of years and they were all very special and happy experiences for me.

There was one other who sailed with me for about five years. His name was George Brewer and he was special also.

I've received my share of honors and awards, but there was one I got during this time that was quite special to me: *Irish America* magazine named me one of the one hundred top Irish businessmen in America. It's not that I was named that thrilled me, but rather who else was on the list. It was a galaxy of business super-stars. My father would have applauded. It was during this period that Barbara and I took another important trip to Ireland. Its purpose was to find my grandparents.

Annual C.I. travel show created by Barbara.

Groundbreaking for the new headquarters with Mayor Leafe and staff.

CI's new headquarters building with our '75 Little Harbor docked in front.

RDO examining original headstone, Bantry Bay, County Cork, Ireland.

22

Finding My Grandparents

hildren usually love their grandparents, and as adults have warm memories of them. When I was young, I felt somewhat cheated because I didn't seem to have any. I mentioned earlier that I knew my grandmother on my mother's side, who had emigrated from about three miles away from Derryvahalla, my father's home.

She was a character, and swapped off living between our home and that of my aunt. It seemed to me that she actually caused some trouble between the two families; in both places, she used to complain about "gouchies" (I think this means ghosts) hiding under her bed.

I learned quite a bit about both my grandfather and my grandmother on my father's side because of the research done by Mr. Daly. For example, I knew my grandfather was a farmer, and a great fiddle player who played at receptions. Apparently my great-grandfather was one of the greatest fiddle players in Ireland, and led the procession of the Leary Glens, as they were known.

As Mr. Daly reported, the oldest son in a family usually didn't marry until he was about forty-five. He then took as a wife a woman of about twenty. Because

RDO with relatives and friends in Bantry Bay, Ireland, cemetery.

I nDil Cuimne ar
Micéál Ó Laoġaire
Corcaiġ
Píobaire
A D'éaġ Anseo
12ú Nollaġ 1986

Ar Deis Dé ġo Raib a Anam

An O'Leary plaque rather recently installed.

of this age difference, my grandmother, the former Mary Harrigan, was a widow who ran the farm for twenty-five years. I wanted to know more about these relatives. I didn't even know where they were buried.

On this trip, Barbara and I planned to find them. Again with the help of Mr. Daly, we trudged through many burial grounds. We finally found the graves where a number of O'Learys were buried, including my grandparents. It was surprisingly close to Derryvahalla, about a mile away.

We were shocked to learn that people in those times were buried in one grave containing sixteen to eighteen bodies. There was some deterioration of the stone, but with a little deciphering it could be determined that this was the resting place of the O'Learys of Derryvahalla.

I wanted to replace that stone with a new one. Mr. Daly said it could probably be arranged but would take some doing. The first step, he said, was to get permission from the current head of the O'Leary clan. I couldn't believe my ears. He offered to drive us to meet him.

We left around seven the next morning. Mr. Daly was quite a driver. After a very speedy ride through glens, valleys, and mountains, we arrived at a pleasant but modest home. I didn't know what to expect when we knocked on the door at ten o'clock.

A very unusual-looking man greeted us. He was elderly and almost mystical in appearance. He had a brogue but spoke excellent English, and had a slight air of nobility about him. He was the leader of the O'Leary clan.

For at least an hour he encouraged Barbara to have a glass of a strong-looking liquid that definitely wasn't tea. I don't really remember, but as I write this, Barbara says she finally had some because she didn't want to be rude. She said it was quite a wake-up call for ten a.m.

We returned to Bantry and the next day worked on the stone's inscription with Mr. Daly and a local artisan. I gave my approval for the graveyard stone and also one for the building my father was born in.

I'm sorry to say that this has not yet been completed, partly because I became very busy with both crises and successes. Mostly, though, I think something happened on the other side. Perhaps writing about it will now motivate me to revitalize the project.

LISHEENS
OVENS
CO. CORK
IRELAND

Dear Richard,

Apologies for the long delay in sending you this letter. I had intended to get it to you before Christmas, but sadly missed that deadline as well.

I have spoken to Tommy Borry regarding the erection of a stone. Tommy suggested that it could be mounted into one of the window openings in the old house into which your father was born. He was born at home. Now that we have the date of birth, the wording on the stone should show this.

Perhaps:

IN MEMORY OF MY FATHER
DANIEL CORNELIUS O'LEARY
BORN IN THIS HOUSE ON
MAY 27, 1889
DIED IN _____ ON _____
AND ALL THE O'LEARY'S WHO LIVE IN THIS LAND
ERECTED BY RICHARD D. O'LEARY, NORFOLK, VIRGINIA, USA
DATE _____

I have also spoken to several members of the O'Leary family—distant relations—and they have no problem with the erection of a new headstone.

Since your visit, another small headstone has been erected to the last O'Leary to be buried in the plot. There is still room for another one. It would be nice to clean up and straighten, and re-do the lettering on the old stone as part of the project.

The lettering on the new headstone in the graveyard could be something like:

IN MEMORY OF MY GRANDPARENTS, CORNELIUS O'LEARY,
WHO DIED ON MARCH 8, 1908, HIS WIFE, MARY, WHO DIED ON
NOVEMBER 3, 1933, AND THE MANY O'LEARY'S INTERRED IN
THIS CEMETERY.
ERECTED BY RICHARD DANIEL O'LEARY,
NORFOLK, VIRGINIA, USA

The headstone cutter may slightly change the wording to fit in with local convention.

What I am planning to do next, Richard, is to get a quotation for the two jobs from W. J. Murphy Monumental Works in Bantry. I will send this to you and then we can go ahead with the order.

I am hoping to visit Mr. Murphy again before the end of next week.

Kathleen and John also send their kindest regards to you. They enjoyed meeting yourself and Barbara in the Hayfield Manor last summer.

I thoroughly enjoyed our day out and look forward to your next visit.

Yours faithfully,

Jerome Daly

ALL ENGINES AHEAD FULL!

AN EXCITING NEW CONCEPT
FOR THE UNIVERSITY AND THE PORT

BY WILLIAM H. WALLACE

Moving into an international leadership role for maritime-related businesses, Old Dominion University is creating a unique International Maritime Port and Logistics Institute with Dr. Geoffrey A. Motte at the helm. This new academic institute came into being as a result of the efforts of many distinguished people in the Hampton Roads community.

The idea originally was suggested by Mr. Richard D. O'Leary who has had a distinguished career in the maritime field. Mr. O'Leary has served in a number of key maritime positions, varying from navigator on the SS United States to an essential post directing the Merchant Marine Academy, to holding leadership positions in government agencies. Mr. O'Leary's prime accomplishment has been the creation of Cruise International, a firm with 33 travel agencies, a division pioneering in cruise ship marketing, and another group operating dinner harbor boats in major American harbors.

In a meeting with President James V. Koch during the late summer of 1990, Mr. O'Leary described Hampton Roads' very high-tech maritime-related industries which vary from sophisticated computer-directed cranes at the container ports, to highly skilled state-of-the-art repair yards, to the astute use of railroads and motor transport for inland port functions. Mr. O'Leary suggested that there were so many rapid developments in technology, for port operations as well as for shipping line management, that an academic institute devoted to maritime-related matters would find a warm welcome from the maritime industry in Hampton Roads. Mr. O'Leary thought that there was an acute need for university level management training and for research and the investigation of new concepts. President Koch concurred and began to investigate the possibilities through the formation of a study group.

The Port and Harbor Study Group was composed of representatives from Civil Engineering, Business Management,

Richard D. O'Leary

Engineering Management, Public Administration, Oceanography, Biology, Economics, Management Information Systems/Decision Sciences. The study group concluded that the University should develop a focal point that could respond to the needs of Hampton Roads and the Commonwealth, the United States and the world, as established by a needs assessment of the field.

In the fall of 1990, Cruise International sold its harbor dinner boat group to an international firm. The dinner boat group wished to honor Mr. O'Leary for his outstanding leadership. With President Koch's cooperation, a fund was created at Old Dominion University to support the initiative proposed by Mr. O'Leary. The original groups of contributors are listed in Figure 1.

President Koch was very fortunate in obtaining the services of James N. Crumbley, who had spent his lifetime in the maritime field culminating with the challenging task of organizing and operating the huge Norfolk International Terminals complex. Well known worldwide in the maritime industry, Mr. Crumbley had retired, but still was very involved in civic work in the community. He agreed to chair a special advisory committee made up of leading executives representing the diverse foreign commerce and port interests in the Hampton Roads area. For ten months, the committee reviewed local, state, regional, national, and international needs in port-related

All engines full ahead.

❧ 23 ❧

Old Dominion University

r. James Koch was the new president of Old Dominion University, which is in Norfolk, Virginia. He was an outgoing person and in my judgment showed early promise as a leader. He began a practice of going out into the community and visiting with people who were prominent in their various fields.

He came to see me and asked if I had any ideas for ways to improve Old Dominion. I suggested that as the college was located in one of the greatest ports in the world, that he might establish a school of port management. Although there were a number of marine educational institutions, two of which I'd been associated with, Maine Maritime and Kings Point, there were no formal educational programs in port management. Port management is a worldwide activity. Later I was told that Dr. Koch had mentioned our conversation to Bev Lawler, one of our board members.

In December 1990 I learned there was to be a special dinner at President Koch's residence. Bev Lawler had organized a fund-raising effort to obtain the seed money for the Richard D. O'Leary Fund for Port and Maritime Management of Old Dominion University. The dinner was a gala affair. Two of our board members, Bev Lawler and Van Cunningham, spoke and made me feel quite proud. In my response, I remember saying that when I first drove across the Hampton Roads Bridge-Tunnel, I no idea of the great adventure that was to come.

I received two magnificent plaques, which sit on my desk here in Maine. The first bears the following inscription:

A Tribute to the
Admiral of the *Spirit*s
We have helped create the
Richard D. O'Leary Fund
for Port and Maritime Management
of Old Dominion University
December 1990

Cyril F. Amos, Jr.
M. Baker, Jr.
John L. Carter
Van H. Cunningham
Robert H. Dickinson
Chester F. Ehrenzeller
Dr. James Garrett
Mr. & Mrs. Robert G. Hofheimer, Jr.
Harold C. Hoy
C. Randolph Hudgins, Jr.
Thomas C. & Elaine M. Kyrus
Bev & Ann Lawler

Dr. Sanford L. Lefcoe
Brian A. Macswain
E. George Middleton, Jr.
James A. Murphy, Jr.
Patrick Thomas Murphy
Colin D. Penny
John L. Roper III
William F. Rountree, Jr.
Thomas M. Vincent
Dr. Jerome H. Weinstein
Walter J. Wilkins

The second reads:

> We support the
> Richard D. O'Leary Fund
> for Port and Maritime Management
> of Old Dominion University
> This is a tip of the hat
> to our favorite wild Irishman
> December 1990

Richard F. Aufinger
Manfred Bloch
Robert F. Boyd
T. J. Broecker
Stephen J. Coplon
R. Stuart Cottrell, Jr.
Van. H. Cunningham
Mary Evelyn Holloman
Bev & Ann Lawler
Robert I. Low

Brian A. Macswain
Gordon B. Marshall
Kevin J. McElroy
John R. Miles
M. Lee Payne
John L. Roper III
F. Coe Sherrard
Alice Rose Vaughan
J. Powell Watson, Jr.

On this list are investors in the original company as well as some who invested in the *Spirit*s and other ventures along the way. I'm enormously grateful to them all.

Assuming command of CINCLANTFLT Detachment-106, the largest Naval Reserve Unit in the country.

24

Life in the
Naval Reserve

y tour of active duty with the Navy comprised some happy years for me. I left the Navy, with some reservation, in Izmir, Turkey, before I went into the Maritime Service. Although I moved on from the Navy, I stayed in the Naval Reserve for twenty-eight years. This was more than an avocation; it was an important part of my life.

Later, when I was on the SS *United States*, we actually had on board a Naval Reserve unit that drilled once each voyage, and I was an active participant.

When I came ashore, I drilled in various units wherever I lived, and advanced to a four-stripe captain. I served as executive officer and commanding officer of three reserve units, a military sealift command unit, and a naval control of shipping unit. I was the executive officer and then commanding officer of the largest Naval Reserve unit in the country. This was the Commander-In-Chief Atlantic detachment, which comprised 130 personnel, including 9 captains. Many of the officers in civilian life held a master's degree or a doctorate.

The Atlantic command was, and I think still is, the largest command in the Navy. The Navy picks about four reserve admirals, known as flag officers, each year. I was quite a hot prospect, as indicated by the following excerpts from my last two fitness reports, both signed by very senior active duty admirals.

K. M. Carr, Vice Admiral, Commander in Chief U.S. Atlantic Command, Norfolk, VA

September 30, 1983

Captain Richard D. O'Leary is the most outstanding Naval Reserve captain attached to this command. His contributions have been so outstanding that this concurrent fitness report is being submitted to ensure that they are recognized and recorded.

As commanding officer of CINCLANTFLT DET 106, a very large and talented unit that augments a diverse number of offices at this headquarters, Captain O'Leary ran his unit smoothly and flawlessly. He accomplished every task assigned during his 2-year command tour, always on time, always in a thorough and professional manner.

Captain O'Leary, a successful businessman and well known community leader, always finds time to take on the many special assignments given him. He seeks responsibility, leads by example and has an infectious, enthusiastic, can-do attitude. He works easily and effortlessly with his officer and enlisted personnel and has quickly gained the respect of the staff's senior officers who view him as a real leader within the Naval Reserve, a person who articulates the Navy's role extremely well, a person who understands the broad picture, an officer who has command presence, a man who has earned his outstanding reputation.

While this fitness report shows Captain O'Leary to be rated one of one, it should be noted that of the two hundred middle and senior grade reserve officers that are attached to CINCLANTFLT, this is the only officer on which a concurrent fitness report is being submitted. He is that deserving. Of the fifty or more Naval Reserve unrestricted line captains that work closely with this staff, many of whom are truly outstanding, the flag officers of this staff are unanimous in recognizing Captain O'Leary as the most outstanding.

I most strongly recommend without reservation Captain O'Leary for promotion to flag now. No one deserves it more. No one is better suited.

J. K. Parker, Rear Admiral, Commander Naval Base,
Norfolk, VA

October 19, 1984

Capt. O'Leary was asked—without advance warning—to assist the COMNAVBASE Norfolk staff planners in the development and preparation of an extremely complicated JCS contingency OPLAN, the reception and onward movement of DOD noncombatant evacuees. He responded quickly to the request and within five days had rearranged his personal schedule to accommodate the SPECDUTRA. Though his tenure as special assistant to the director, operations, plans, and security was brief, he was able to produce a comprehensive and workable plan.

Capt. O'Leary is a perceptive and highly respected officer who relates well with his subordinates, peers, and superiors. He is articulate, persuasive in speech, and is an effective writer. He is an exceptionally competent officer capable of achieving both operational and administrative objectives. His physical appearance is outstanding and he meets the height/weight and physical fitness goals of the Navy. He is most strongly recommended for early promotion to Commodore, future command assignments, and retention in the Naval Reserve.

This reporting senior in 43 years of active naval service has observed hundreds of reserve officers in many environments. Never have I seen a senior reserve officer who impressed me more with his broad-based talents, love of Navy, and desire to contribute to the one Navy concept. Richard O'Leary is a superb officer, a gentleman without peer, and a stalwart in the community who would be a magnificent representative for the Navy as a flag officer. He should be selected now.

In spite of these reports, I learned I didn't make it when I received the following letter from Richard Young, Commodore, USNR-R.

8 March 1984

The new Naval Reserve Commodore list is out, as you know. While I am in no way saying that any selectee should not be on the list, I want you to know that I was extremely disappointed not to see your name there.

I have not talked to, nor do I intend to talk to, any of the members on the Board, but I think you know that in my opinion, you are one of the finest officers with whom I have ever been associated.

Your years of dedicated service to the Navy and Naval Reserve have been simply outstanding. I know from my many personal contacts that your talent and expertise are extremely well regarded by both active and Naval Reserve people.

I also want you to know that this letter is not a letter of sympathy or a letter implying that it's time to move on. To the contrary, in addition to trying to thank you and to make sure you understand how appreciated your fine work of the past has been, it is intended to keep you in there. Lightning could strike next year, and even if it doesn't, your time, talent, and energy are still very much needed.

I want to keep you at work. I am going to assume that you are going to keep producing. I hope that we can get together the next time I am in Norfolk. I plan to arrive the evening of March 21, and will be there through Sunday evening, March 25. I believe we have a meeting scheduled for late Thursday afternoon on the MINI-MOB exercise. Please let me know if there is a good time when we can get together while I am there.

Years later I was hosting a luncheon on my yacht for Mayor Mason Andrews and his wife, Sabine, and Admiral Jack Parker and his wife, Jackie. Admiral Parker was commanding officer of the Norfolk naval base and was on the selection board when I was considered. Admiral Parker told me that I actually had been selected. The selection boards are usually made up of four regular Navy admirals and four Reserve admirals. I had heard rumors that there was some inappropriate politicking by the Reserve officers, and the secretary of the Navy had disbanded the board and nullified the results. I know nothing more of the details. I would be less than honest if I said I wasn't disappointed, but it was a long time ago.

Barbara has always said this may have been for the best, because it would have distracted me from managing my company. She and I had visited Israel as guests of that country's government, and I'd become quite interested in the Israeli reserve system. If I was

Saluting Admiral Jack Parker, commanding officer of the Norfolk naval base.

selected, I had planned to visit Israel at my expense and further study its system with the view of seeing if some of the best procedures would work here. Barbara was probably right. This may have very well affected the growth and success of Cruise Ventures, Inc.

A member of the Naval Reserve in this country drills either one night a week or one weekend a month and two weeks each year. The pay is modest, as are the retirement benefits, and reservists are subject to almost immediate recall. I often thought—in fact, I know—that some people did it just for the money and the retirement benefits. This was never the case with me, and I drilled for some four years without pay: I did it simply because I loved the Navy.

Former Chrysler home at the U.S. Merchant Marine Academy.

25

A Nostalgic Return to Kings Point

 ater, after having been in Norfolk for a number of years, Barbara and I had an interesting little adventure. Walter Chrysler, Jr., had moved to Norfolk because his wife, Jean, was originally from there. He had grown up in the Chrysler mansion, which is now the administration building of the U.S. Merchant Marine Academy.

I was surprised to receive an invitation to lunch from Mr. Chrysler, who was well known in Norfolk because he had moved his art collection from Provincetown, Massachusetts, to Norfolk and established it as part of the Norfolk Museum, which was renamed the Chrysler Museum.

I learned at the luncheon that he wanted to have the largest of three beautiful Italian fireplaces from the administration building moved to the Chrysler Museum. He thought I might be able to accomplish this. I listened attentively, but wasn't encouraging.

I ended up writing a perfunctory letter to the Maritime Administration in Washington. In response, I received a perfunctory letter saying no.

Mr. Chrysler called and asked if I would pursue it directly with officials of the academy. I contacted Admiral King and my old friend Captain Paul Krinsky, who was now the academic dean, and worked out a proposal of sorts. The academy would let him have one of the smaller fireplaces if he would finance the restoration of the ornate ceiling of the main building. This generated enough interest that Mr. Chrysler asked if I would accompany him to New York and meet with academy officials. He had not returned to the site since his family donated it to the government in 1941.

The academy made some very special arrangements. The main dining room, with its twenty-five-foot ceilings and huge fireplace, was being used for important meetings, such as the Congressional Board of Visitors.

With much thought and care, a wonderful luncheon was planned for Mr. Chrysler's return home. Barbara and I joined him for the flight to New York, where we were met by academy vehicles. The day was splendid and we spent hours touring and listening to interesting facts about the building and grounds. A great deal of lore had developed through the years, much of it inaccurate.

The dean of admission's office, on the second floor, turned out to have been Mr. Chrysler's bedroom. It opened into a secret hiding place where he used to look down on the gala parties. The superintendent's office, with the ramps, hadn't been his father's bedroom; I believe he said it was his mother's. Adjacent to this office and my old one was a beautiful boardroom with an elaborate bathroom where a barber used to give haircuts to Admiral McLintock and me. Mr. Chrysler told us his father would sit on the privy and work on the design of the Airflow automobile, which wasn't a success. It was a fascinating day, and we had a wonderful time peeking into the private lives of some very famous people.

Around this time, we had a grand opening of our new waterfront headquarters. It was quite a guest list for Norfolk. It included Walter Chrysler, Jr., and Admiral McLintock, who had retired.

When Mr. Chrysler met the admiral, he talked about his project and told him I was trying to help out. Admiral McLintock said, "No problem: Dick will take care of this for you." Oops!

About a week later, Mr. Chrysler again invited me for lunch. He had a new offer. He told me Chrysler men didn't usually live to a ripe old age and then he offered to put in his will a 300,000-dollar bequest for the fireplace. There was no mention of the ceiling. I passed this along, but to my knowledge, nothing ever happened. Barbara and I, however, quite enjoyed it all.

26

Ten Year Club

t about this time I established what I called a Ten Year Club, obviously for people who had been with the company at least a decade. I wanted the details to be a surprise, so I didn't tell anyone what I had in mind, not even Barbara. It wasn't easy keeping it a secret, as my plan involved flying some people to Norfolk. We met on one of the *Spirit* ships, where I thanked them and presented an engraved pen set to each. I followed this with an attractive certificate. Both gestures were greeted warmly.

But then I explained that nobody knew what I was going to do next because it was still in my head. I then told the accounting department to cut a check for 1,000 dollars for each of them—that certainly got their attention. Then I said I'd arranged for us all to go to the Harbor Club that noon for champagne and wine and to talk about the old days.

The whole event was a hit, and we made it a company tradition. We added some travel to the program, and in subsequent years we went to Williamsburg, New York, Jamaica, Maine, Rome and other nice destinations. They tell me their favorite was our home in Maine.

The Ten Year Club had sixty-eight members, mostly from the Norfolk area. We then created a Twenty Year Club, with about twenty-five members, and even a Thirty Year Club, which boasted a handful of great people.

As I write this I am reminded of a former secretary of mine. She was very efficient and officious. She wanted to send Barbara home one day for wearing a sundress to work, in violation of company rules. Prior to the trip to Rome, Barbara and I went to Ireland for a few days and joined the group at London's Heathrow Airport. I was dressed informally and had mud on my shoes. She came over to me and said, "Go clean or change your shoes. You really look like an Irishman."

❧ 27 ❧

Troubles in the Airways

used to think the airlines were well-managed companies. That was a long, long time ago. Now I'm convinced they're among the worst.

For a while, Warren Buffett was on the board of US Airways. When he left, it was reported that he said the best thing for investors would have been if somebody had shot the Wright brothers down when they were at Kitty Hawk.

I think the net aggregate result of all airline activity is a loss. It's either famine or feast for companies, such as ours, that do a good part of the sales and marketing for the airlines.

Years back, because we were so big, we received excellent compensation. Our commissions were fifteen percent, and in certain situations they were even more. Then, because of heavy losses, the airlines initiated a program of gradual commission cuts. They began with small cuts that shocked us. Then they really got shocking. Over just a few years, in gradual steps they cut the commission rate to zero. This forced travel companies to charge fees and collect directly from their customers. Waves of horror hit the industry and our air departments. We had to lean more heavily on our commercial operations, as companies would pay a fee to have their commercial travel work undertaken. In most cases, this is more cost effective than a company doing the work itself, as airlines can offer deals to an agency for the business because of economies of scale and automation.

Similarly, the airlines seem never to be able to decide whether they want to charter their planes. More than once we created programs using the planes of a particular airline and when results looked favorable, they'd increase the charter fee and try to do it themselves, usually unsuccessfully.

It's a difficult business; most airlines lose money most of the time. A company must be flexible and nimble. As they say, change is the law of life, but this business is over the top.

We have remained in the business by concentrating on commercial accounts. Among those we've held for many years are NASA, Wright-Patterson Air Force Base, Joy Global, the Securities and Exchange Commission, and Hickam Air Force Base in Hawaii.

The most negative effect in the industry has been on retail travel shops, but travel agents are like ants: resourceful and almost impossible to stamp out.

In spite of these difficulties, I opened a separate company in Naples, Florida, called CI Consulting, and it's done quite well, with four offices. Its success is the result of the local leadership of Dina Babka, particularly good chemistry in the personnel mix, and the demographics of the city.

At the inception of the parent company, we marketed only cruise ships. As mentioned earlier, we didn't get into the travel agency business for several years. Like many other industries back then, the business was primitive by today's standards. Our entrance consisted of one person writing air tickets by hand. The industry transformed itself and now involves highly specialized and technical equipment. Because of good in-house decision making, we grew from that modest beginning to become one of the largest and most successful travel companies in the country.

This is a good place to acknowledge the work of Kevin McElroy, who has managed and expanded this part of the business for years. He's a very capable, hands-on executive who has contributed to the overall company as well as to this division. CI earned a lot of awards and commendations that are listed in the appendix.

Joe Good, another vice president, who I'm sad to say is now deceased, made many contributions and was a gifted leader in the field of government travel.

❧ 28 ❧

Sale of the *Spirits*

bout a dozen years after we entered the business, the *Spirit*s were attracting a lot of favorable attention. We had been approached a couple of times about selling all divisions of the company.

We received an offer through Bear Stearns to merge with a company that owned the Yellow Pages of Israel. The plan was to have the new entity build stations that would enable passengers to go below the sea surface and observe marine life. Barbara and I met some interesting people and had several great dinners in New York, but I wasn't ready.

We then were approached in a letter to sell the *Spirit* fleet to a boat company in San Francisco owned by Terry McCrea. The offer was interesting and contained a very attractive multiple of earnings. In talking with Terry, he suggested that I'd feel better with some change in my jeans.

We entered into a due-diligence exercise with his company. It took about six weeks. I was firm in my resistance to any changes because I wasn't eager to sell. Some complicated multiple-level financing was created. In any case, the financing plan failed by one vote because the chairman of a Chicago bank didn't like ships.

I had gotten used to the idea of having some change in my jeans, but we never solicited buyers. A little more than a year later, I got a phone call from a man with a French accent. It was J. P. Cuny, the president of the leisure division of Sodexho (now Sodexo), a huge company located in Paris. He indicated that they wanted to explore purchasing the entire fleet of *Spirit*s, which now consisted of thirteen vessels.

This was January, and we arranged to meet in Norfolk in February. That began a complicated process that would take eight months. Sodexho also owned a fleet of boats that operated on the river Seine. One problem arose almost immediately. It was something I was familiar with: the Jones Act of 1920, also called the cabotage laws, prohibited the sale of ships built in America to a foreign company for operation in America.

The Jones Act was highly supported by labor unions and was designed to protect American ships, railroads, and trucking companies from foreign ships operating between two American ports.

My cursory investigation indicated that we couldn't get around these laws. To me, it was an open-and-shut case. I met with J. P. Cuny and his associates in Norfolk. This was followed a few weeks later by a meeting at the old Pan Am Building in New York with Sodexho executives and some attorneys from Ropes & Gray, a large Boston law firm. They seemed confident that we could go forward. I wasn't confident at all, but agreed to go ahead.

The due-diligence process began in Norfolk with Sodexho financial people going through our records and visiting each of the cities in which the *Spirit*s

The Spirit of Norfolk *approaches headquarters to say good-bye after the change of ownership.*

operated. I had numerous meetings with J. P. in Norfolk, Boston, and Paris. Barbara and I even attended a boat christening on the Seine and met Brigitte Bardot and her dog.

I came to know some of the people at Ropes & Gray. The firm specializes in foreign transactions, mostly European. They're open most of the night because of time differences.

The negotiations settled into a group of four or five from Sodexho and four or five of our people. Sometimes when we were convened, I would leave for a while and the French would leave too. They really wanted to negotiate only with those whom they perceived to be the decision makers. This made for some tough sessions.

But J. P. and I became and remained friends. Barbara and I visited with him and his family in Paris several times.

As the months went by, the negotiations and the work went on. We were into the summer and the Sodexho executives and its president visited us at our home in Ogunquit. The president actually swam in the ocean and caught a plane back to Paris that night with salt still clinging to him. We had a wonderful time together and a great lobster lunch at Barnacle Billy's.

As the summer went on, I began to appreciate Ropes & Gray's attempts to overcome the Jones Act restrictions. Its attorneys put together an almost unbelievably complicated arrangement. It involved two banks, a Hawaii leasing company,

A two a.m. toast on board our yacht after completion of negotiations for the sale of the Spirits. *Barbara and I were joined by Chuck Payne, our attorney, and Bob Low, our CPA, who had both been with us since the beginning.*

partnerships, and tons of legal documents. But I guess it worked, and I became a believer that smart lawyers can accomplish almost anything.

The closing took place at the offices of Ropes & Gray in Boston. There was a document room with what seemed like hundreds of documents. It was locked and had a guard. Some negotiations were still going on.

We were ready to start signing papers at about one a.m. When I sat down, my bracelet got caught in the table so I couldn't sign. A couple of people got it loose and we proceeded. At nine the next morning, Barbara and I left our hotel. As we drove by Rowes Wharf, workmen were already painting out the C.I. logos. We headed home to Maine, and I was *Spirit*-less.

However, I am proud to say that all of those ships are still operating successfully in the original cities where we introduced them.

PART FIVE

❧ 29 ❧

Wild Thing

*L*ife was going quite smoothly. We needed something exciting, and got control of a *Wild Thing*. This is not a success story.

The *Wild Thing* was a vessel constructed something like a big barge but with great engine power that could drive it at more than thirty knots. A father-and-son team who lived in Virginia Beach built it. They had tried to use it there but were not successful. They'd offered to charter it to us but I'd declined. They then moved it to St. Thomas, in the Caribbean, where they were attempting to take passengers from the many visiting cruise ships for a snorkeling adventure. They would run it off St. John and the passengers would go snorkeling with supplied gear. There was even a nurse on board. On the way back to St. Thomas, they'd open the rum, then turn on the music and the speed. It truly was a wild thing.

But they weren't doing well, and offered it to me again. Bob Low, our CPA and usually a very conservative chap, was almost their advocate. With a good deal of hubris, I then decided they didn't know what they were doing. I thought about

The Wild Thing *with my sailboat in the Caribbean.*

how easy it would be for us to get passengers because of my connections with top executives in the shipping lines.

We thought a change in concept was also necessary. We came up with the idea of doing a circumnavigation of the island of St. Thomas.

Despite the great lack of success we had with the first *Spirit of Norfolk/ Miami*, we thought—no, we knew—we'd soon have the *Wild Thing* under control. It seems I hadn't learned my lessons about old boats.

We acquired a couple of new contracts with cruise lines, but the boat itself was more than too much for us. We experienced every conceivable problem that can befall a watercraft. We had groundings, engine failures, incidents caused by rum, even a propeller fell off. After employing divers to search for the propeller for days, I realized it was time to move on. The *Wild Thing* was too wild for us.

❧ 30 ❧

Employee Stock Ownership Plan

significant date in our company, and of course for all other companies as well, was September 11, 2001. For us, business came to a stop. We had to take some drastic action. We laid off forty people in our Norfolk operation; the rest were put on a four-day workweek. We then began, along with everyone else, the long, slow process of first holding on to and then regrowing our business.

I took myself off the payroll and had the payroll department secretly hold the money. I then personally gave all our employees their normal Christmas bonuses. We didn't have our usual Christmas party in a hotel ballroom. We gathered in our commercial travel working space, which was crowded and intimate. We held hands and sang, "Let there be peace on earth and let it begin with me." This tradition continued in the company at least until I retired, and also in my family. It was one of the warmest memories I have of my thirty-four years with C.I.

Through the years I'd never really encouraged any feelers from people who wanted to buy the company. The whole thing was personal to me; I loved our employees and they were like family.

I read about a rather new procedure that accomplished the partial or full turnover of ownership of a company to its employees. An Employee Stock Ownership Plan (ESOP) is a government plan to turn employees into employee-owners. I read a lot about this very complicated and technical process and it had some features that appealed to me. The main one was that it offered a plan to liquefy some portion of the equity that had accumulated in the company and establish an incentive-based retirement program, making employees beneficial stockowners in the company where they worked. This was not a simple matter and I studied, as did our staff, the details.

I'd like to interject a small, very personal note here. I mentioned earlier that I was never much of a golfer, but I did play at it. My wife and I were participating in a golf mixer at the Cape Neddick Country Club, which is in Ogunquit. The people we played with were a charming couple named Iris and Bernard Snyder.

A few days later, Bernie called me and said he'd like to play golf with me. I couldn't imagine why. However, it turned out to be a wonderful relationship and we continued to play together for about fifteen years. As Bernie would put it, "We were made for each other—both bad."

Bernie was a New York and Boston tax attorney and had taught a number of courses. We had many stimulating conversations during our years of golf struggles. When he heard that I was contemplating doing an ESOP, he handed me a book and said I might be interested in it. I was. It was one of the first books written about ESOPs; the author was Bernard Snyder.

The decision was made to proceed, and we engaged Menke & Associates, of San Francisco, the largest ESOP firm in the country, to assist us. Menke was invaluable during all the planning and execution.

Although I was wholly involved in the design and implementation of this plan, and have now participated some five times, I'm not expert enough to present what's entailed in a way that would be of interest to the average reader, so I will just offer some highlights. I'll try to keep this as nontechnical as possible.

Because it's a federal program, everything must be done in a very circumspect manner. The company's stock must be appraised and valued by a government-approved but independent appraiser.

The stock can then be purchased using retained earnings or by creating an ESOP loan. In the case of C.I., we used some of each. We had very good credit ratings with a number of banks. When we sold the *Spirits*, we paid off about 32 million dollars in loans to a number of banks. They were all sorry to have it end because we had never missed or even been late with a payment. The loan we created for the plan would be paid off with future earnings and fifty percent guaranteed by the original stockholders. A considerable amount of cash from the company's treasury, plus the loan, was used to buy the stock from the current owners and put in a trust for all employees. The employees each received stock in their names, the amount depending on various factors, such as salary and length of service. An ESOP committee, made up of employees, was established to administer the trust and the stock.

One of the principal advantages of the plan is that if at least thirty percent of the company's outstanding stock has been sold to the ESOP and the proceeds are reinvested in the securities of American companies, the sale and interest are tax-free. Federal statistics show that ESOP companies tend to be eight to eleven percent more profitable than their non-ESOP counterparts.

At the time of this step, I hadn't thought much beyond completing the first trench. On November 12, 1996, we gathered our board and investors and all the Norfolk employees for a gala reception and presentation at the Chrysler Museum. It was a wonderful experience, and the employees now owned about a third of the company. This cost them absolutely nothing in money or benefits. Also, the money they had in their profit-sharing plan was theirs to keep. This was substantial because they had been receiving fifteen percent of the company's profits for a good number of years.

What actually happened with the ESOP was that after we paid off the loan, we implemented the process again, to transfer more ownership. I was now looking to the future, and formulated a plan so that one hundred percent ownership of the company would coincide with my retirement, and that's what happened.

I also created the Richard and Barbara O'Leary Employee Benefit Plan, which I funded personally. This plan will receive more money upon my death. I write this section not to point out my good nature, but rather because it's history. Some will see me as a man who cared about his people, and I will proudly accept that compliment.

As I wrote earlier, I believe that for an entrepreneur to be successful, he or she must take care of the people who show their belief in him (or her) by investing and risking their money, and also take care of the people who work in the enterprise. I have tried to do both.

This makes me think of my father, who didn't have much to give but who gave all he had. I've been fortunate to inherit a number of his characteristics. I know he would have heartily approved of what I've done to take care of my people. His teachings—beginning with "Be good to people"—have guided me throughout my career.

The following letter from Georgia-Anna Burton shows what a difference our plan made in the lives of our employees.

1-24-07

Richard,

Thinking back over the years I have spent with C.I. many many events stick out in my mind—the one major one that has made the biggest impact on my life was when you announced the formation of the ESOP—now 12 years later, and being over 55 years I was able to diversify funds, open an IRA last year and this year I was able to withdraw the money and use it for a down payment on my very first home—my dream, the American dream has finally come true.

Thanks to you and your vision and your business sense it has made a difference in my life, my daughter's and my grandson's too. I will be eternally grateful.

Thank you, Richard—

My best to you and Barbara,

     G. A.

     With great appreciation
     Georgia-Anna Burton
     Hampton/Peninsula
     C.I. Travel

Retirement

 now busied myself with plans for how to leave the company I had led and loved for so many years. An integral component was to complete the hundred-percent transfer of the ownership of the company to the employees on the same day I retired.

Each year in July we held a company meeting of the employees in the Norfolk area. The group comprised about 150 people: the core employees of the company and key employees from other cities, whom we flew in. It was always a party atmosphere. Many awards were presented, such as Employee of the Year, Office of the Year, and monetary gifts, along with induction of new members to the Ten Year Club. I took the opportunity to speak to them emphasizing our core values, including the philosophy of "doing a little more than people expect" from back in Webster Junior High School, when I was thirteen.

For at least two years before my retirement, I stressed the factors that had brought us from nowhere to our present position. I also announced my retirement date and told them that after that day I would no longer be involved in the company. I said I didn't want to be a person who comes back and gives advice

Norfolk employees at the 2004 company meeting.

or criticism. When I would mention this to people privately, they would reply, "You'll never be able to keep away after thirty-four years." I would respond by gently reminding them that I had done just that with the SS *United States*, the U.S. Merchant Marine Academy, the Port Authority, the *Spirit* organization, and in fact every other place I had ever worked.

I've taken the liberty of including some of my remarks at the last company meeting, one year before my retirement.

> I would like to ask you to think about a little company that was located just a few blocks from here, down in a windowless basement with very few people and limited funds, and all kinds of difficulty.
>
> We lost the one ship contract we had because our fellow travel agents were boycotting us. How did that company come from there to manage 350 cruises on 26 different cruise ships from 20 different companies, the only company in the U.S. to do that kind of business except for shipping companies? And then go on to build a fleet of 12 *Spirit*-class vessels employing over 2,000 people, buying 500,000 pounds of food at a time, and moving 17,000 people per day and 1.5 million people per year. Then develop what is arguably the best travel show in the country and then go on to become the 36th-largest travel company out of 25,000 and service some of the most prestigious accounts in the U.S.

I will tell you how we did this. We did this by being very selective about the people we engaged. I don't mean just executives but people at every level, especially people who dealt with our customers. And we tried to inculcate in them a notion or a belief that to do more than people expect you to do is the secret to success. And we watched costs closely and made sure that new projects had to have a short-term benefit as well as a long-term benefit.

And, lastly, we built a close-knit, cohesive management team that managed with vision, boldness, and determination. It is my hope that those traditions will continue far into the foreseeable future.

When I leave this company it will be very sad for me, but I will not be the kind of person who comes back and offers advice or criticism. It is not in my nature, but I will keep one share of stock so you will have to write to me.

In my last year, I was busy completing the last portion of the ESOP and picking a successor, a new CEO, and a new board of directors.

The day finally arrived, July 26, 2005. Much more work had gone into preparation for this day by our advertising department, law firm, accounting firm, public relations people, and Barbara than I was aware of. That afternoon I held my final board meeting as chairman. I selected experienced and dependable Kevin McElroy to be the new CEO. The board would consist of several new outsiders and two rank-and-file employees. Don Mayer, my son-in-law, was elected chairman of the board. We passed a number of routine resolutions necessary for such an occasion. Goodman and Company, our CPA firm, presented me with a framed steel plaque showing the company's financial record. The company had lost money only twice in thirty-four years. Also, each original investor in the parent company had received approximately 496,000 dollars for their investment of 5,000 dollars.

People who invested in some or all of the *Spirits* and other ventures made a good deal more, but that could not be shown on this plaque. The plaque also contained a curve showing that our profit averaged fourteen percent per year, greatly outpacing the Dow Jones Industrial average and the S&P 500.

The new board passed a resolution naming me Chairman of the Board, Emeritus. It was presented to me later that evening framed and with twelve "whereas" paragraphs extolling the company's achievements.

It was time to thank and say good-bye to my board members and to my attorney and CPA, who had done such wonderful work through the years.

Our office headquarters were then in the Norfolk World Trade Center. After the *Spirit* sale, we sold our building to People for the Ethical Treatment of Animals (PETA), which used it as its headquarters.

It was almost time to change clothes and go downstairs to the Town Point Club. We had close to 250 guests. Among them were investors and many employees, past and present. Some former employees had come from as far away as New York, Florida, Ohio, Massachusetts, Montana, and the six contiguous cities of Hampton Roads. Seven mayors of Hampton Roads were at a special table that included four former mayors of Norfolk and the present mayors of Virginia Beach and Portsmouth. At our table were Mayor Paul Fraim, of Norfolk; Robert Dickinson, president of Carnival Cruise Lines, who flew up from Miami; Len Tyler, president of the Maine Maritime Academy, who traveled from Castine, Maine; Paul Krinsky, former superintendent of the U.S. Merchant Marine Academy, who flew in from New York City; and Monsignor Pitt, substituting for Bishop Walter F. Sullivan, who had undergone surgery two days earlier. (Bishop Sullivan and I had cruised together thirty-three years earlier.) Also at our table was one of the best friends I've ever had, John Roper, and his wife, Jinnie. To add a sad note to this, John was experiencing early Alzheimer's disease and I seated him at my side to try to be a little protective of him. And, of course, once again, I almost forgot to mention my Barbara.

It's not possible to list all the guests and dignitaries, but there was another very special table, the one with our seven daughters and their husbands. Danielle had come from New York, Megan from Washington, and Lauren, Leslie, Michele, Stephanie, and Dione from Virginia Beach.

At another table, right beside mine, sat Judge and Mrs. Robert Doumar, Mr. and Mrs. Walter Ray, Mr. and Mrs. Lee Payne, Mr. and Mrs. George Dragas, and Mr. and Mrs. Walter Galliford.

The evening began with the guests chatting and imbibing; I abstained, though, as I was too excited. Barbara, who was the voice and face of C.I., had produced a film. (She produced many ads and radio spots during her more than thirty years with the company, and was even the personality in many of them. She carefully chronicled on film the events and history of all the years of the company.)

Unbelievably, our library of films seemed to have been lost after the sale of our building, but this did not deter her. With incredible tenacity, she collected news clips from TV stations and snippets of less-than-perfect films and put forth an amazing product. It documented much of the company's history in a very enjoyable format. It contained our musical theme and footage of important business events, company picnics, and the beginning of the Ten Year Club. It featured many employees in charming scenes. She arranged to have built a four-screen format that reached everyone in the room.

The twenty-minute musical film opened the after-dinner festivities and was a hit. This was followed by a number of speakers. Tom Vincent, senior vice president of Ogilvy & Mather advertising agency, spoke about my solicitation of ships from Cunard Line; Len Tyler spoke about my early days at Maine Maritime; Paul Krinsky spoke about our long association and friendship; and Bob Dickinson was Bob Dickinson—he can be a very funny guy, and he was.

Mayor Paul Fraim offered some words that were very special to me. I have included a letter containing some of them.

The podium presentation included not only the resolution naming me Chairman of the Board, Emeritus, but also a similar one outlining Barbara's achievements.

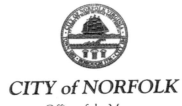

CITY of NORFOLK

Office of the Mayor

Paul D. Fraim,
Mayor

Dear Richard,

It is with many fond memories and not a little nostalgia that I offer you my warmest congratulations on the occasion of your retirement from CI Travel/Cruise International.

Your lifelong passion for the romance of the sea and the lure of world travel is aptly reflected in your rich and varied career. U.S. Naval Officer, a merchant mariner, navigator on the luxury liner *S.S. United States*, Commandant of Kings Point Merchant Marine Academy and founder and patriarch of CI Travel/Cruise International, I know there has to be a book somewhere in your future.

You have also been a good and true friend to the City of Norfolk. As I remember, it was not long after the opening of The Waterside and Town Point Park as pioneer projects for downtown's revitalization, you came to the Council with the idea of operating a dinner cruise ship out of Otter Berth. This proved a perfect match for both Spirit Cruises and the city as the *Spirit of Norfolk* quickly became a waterfront icon. That it remains so to this day, and that you nurtured the idea into a thriving business, is a tribute to your vision.

As your travel business began to experience robust growth – ultimately becoming the 36th largest in the nation – you could have gone anywhere, but you chose to build your corporate headquarters here and remain in Norfolk. We have not forgotten your faith in the city, and very much appreciate the contributions you have made to our success.

As you prepare to begin this new chapter in your life, I hope you would consider allowing us to call upon your wisdom and experience should the need arise. In closing, please know that you and Barbara have my very best wishes for all the future has to offer.

Sincerely,

Paul D. Fraim
Mayor

Charles Payne gave me seven beautifully bound books containing the minutes from all the board meetings over the history of the company. Kevin McElroy presented a beautiful book called *A Special Tribute to Richard Daniel O'Leary*. It consisted of letters from wonderful friends and many incredible color photographs. Like this book, it highlights my life with letters and photographs. It's one of my most valued possessions. Barbara clandestinely conceived and created that book in association with personnel from our advertising agency. It seems impossible to me that they kept it a secret.

Mayor Oberndorf, of Virginia Beach, designated July 27, 2005, as Richard and Barbara O'Leary Day in that city.

Reproduced here are the comments from Melissa Lindsay, director of human resources, who spoke for the employees. Also included are two letters from Lee Payne, a former chairman of the board of United Virginia Bank, who spoke for the investors. They aren't verbatim accounts of what he said because I don't have copies, but they are, I think, representative.

> So, Richard and Barbara are retiring. I'm not sure any of us believed that this day would arrive. We all thought retirement was something they thought about, talked about, threatened, and sometimes prayed for but would never do. In our ideal world, Richard would always be at the helm with Barbara by his side. For thirty-three years he has made us feel safe, secure, ready to take on and slay any dragon that crossed our path.
>
> How do I express what Richard and Barbara have meant, not to just me, but to all of C.I.'s employees? It's difficult to narrow down all that they are in a few hundred words or five minutes, since Richard said that's all the time I have.
>
> Richard and Barbara O'Leary are C.I. Travel. One is synonymous with the other. Richard is the backbone. From him we get our strength, determination, and courage to succeed in all our endeavors. Barbara is our shining light. Her beauty, strength, grace, and genuine kindness have long made C.I. a better company to work for and with.
>
> I was given advice from many on things to include in my speech. The most common was to tell some funny stories about Richard. My first reaction was that he isn't really a funny guy, but as I started writing I started remembering. Richard calling to Barbara from his office (three offices away); in fact, thinking back, that's how he calls all of us. His astonishment when he learned after twenty years that Brenda's name was really Cheryl. That's okay; where Richard is concerned, we all answer to anything. There's the annual do-not-make-eye-contact-with-Richard the day of the Christmas party or you'll end up doing the blessing at the party.

Some of us have gone to great lengths to avoid that. A million memories and he is funnier than I thought.

What is it that we the employees want to thank them for? I'm sure if you asked Richard, he would tell you that it was his company. Certainly, the ESOP is a wonderful thing, but he's given us something better than that. He's given us each other.

Thirty-three years ago Richard didn't just start a company; he started a family. As I read the RSVP list for this party, I came to the realization of how true this is. Employees who left the company, years ago, have made their way back, some from great distances, to share this night with us.

What makes us come to work each day? We don't all love our jobs every day. Believe me, there are many days when I wanted to throw Richard's checkbook and him off the balcony. So, what is it? What keeps us here? It isn't salaries, fancy offices, or perks. It's the environment that Richard and Barbara have created here. Each office, each department contains our family away from family. Our coworkers are the ones we work with, laugh with, cry with, celebrate our successes and mourn our failures with. And being a company of mostly women, we can run the gamut of these emotions every day. We come to work for more than our paycheck. We're here for each other. Our teamwork and loyalty to each other and this company are what make C.I. so great. This is the legacy you're leaving us, and we love you all the more for it.

So, Richard and Barbara, as our lives take different directions, we pray that the rest of your days are filled with sunshine and laughter. We hope that your boat trips with Richard the captain and Barbara the first mate will be with a minimum of mutinies and always calm seas. We will think of you often and tell stories about you for years.

Richard, you've given us strength, and faith in ourselves and in those we work with, so that no matter what lies ahead we will thrive as a company. You've taught us how to succeed. I want you to know that you have left us in good hands. So, don't worry about us. We'll be all right, and know that we will never forget you.

I will never forget you.

I meant every word.

Love,
Melissa

Dear Richard,

My personal career in banking covers almost 50 years and in that period of time I have had the opportunity to meet many corporate executives. Periodically I think to myself about the many outstanding people whom I have had the pleasure of knowing and, although the many outstanding participants change from time to time, your name always stays at the top of this list. Your ability to see an opportunity to create corporate values and to develop a committed staff places you high in my opinion and in a very unique position among all my current and past acquaintances. It is difficult to say this in public, but believe me I mean it with great sincerity. You are a remarkable executive.

With all good wishes,
M. Lee Payne

A Brief Memory of an Extraordinary Cruise Lasting Thirty-Four Years

John Roper and I have, over the years, participated in several financial crap shoots, and when he called me to hear a proposal in early 1972, I, of course, responded. I forthwith met the most ingratiating and imaginative group of thieves and vagabonds I have ever encountered. Richard, of course, was an unknown entity, but with Roper's encouragement I joined the crowd and was subsequently elected to the board. Meeting in a damp snake pit in the basement of an abandoned warehouse on Bute Street was a bit of a come-down, but Richard always had the charismatic ability to spin a golden web for the future. And in spite of a few corporate hiccups such has certainly occurred. I looked back with pleasure through a full file cabinet of information and can only say that this has been the most remarkable sleigh ride I have ever experienced. In spite of the current hesitancy, it is a real pleasure that Norfolk—finally—is proceeding to make a major cruise terminal a reality.

In 1985 I wrote a congratulatory letter to Richard, and a copy is enclosed herewith. All I can add is an acknowledgement of his major contribution to his adopted city and my pleasure in being along for the ride.

Many thanks, congratulations, and Good Luck!
Lee

Needless to say, I sat there with a heart full of love and gratitude. Bob Dickinson, who stayed with Barbara and me that night, called me from Atlanta the next day. He told me he had never experienced a room that felt so full of love.

I also felt great gratitude to all the people who had worked with me and helped me. I felt gratitude to God and to my parents. The love in that room, I assure you, was two-way.

I walked to the microphone with a very spiritual feeling. I then made some rather short comments, at least for me. I thanked all the different categories of people present. My most heartfelt thanks, however, were for the two groups I've mentioned more than once already: my investors and my employees.

I'm a very strong believer in capitalism. I suggested to the room that our little company represented capitalism at its very best. We had taken some new ideas and sold them to a group of people willing to take a risk for the potential of profiting. This is classic capital formation. We nurtured and developed the ideas through adversity and good fortune, then took steps to transfer ownership, in our case, to the wonderful people who had done the work. This is classic capitalism, I said.

I went to take my seat and was surprised and embarrassed because something impromptu occurred. I was embarrassed because I thought it was time for this to end. Father Vince Connery, the young priest who had such an influence on Barbara's and my life, called on our seven daughters to come up. I protested a little, but we prayed and sang "Let There Be Peace on Earth." I really didn't mind, and I don't think the guests did either.

Then it was over. Thirty-three, or more nearly thirty-four, years of adventure, hardship, failure, and high success. I think this is another way of saying *life*, and I enjoyed it all.

𝕻roclamation

Whereas: *Richard O'Leary founded CI Travel in 1972 and was joined by his wife, Barbara, in 1978; and*

Whereas: *CI Travel grew to become a $175 million company with 49 locations in 12 states and Washington, D.C.; and*

Whereas: *The company has won numerous awards and honors both in Hampton Roads and in the travel industry as a whole; and*

Whereas: *CI Travel's success has been passed on to its employees, who became 100 percent owners of the company on April 1, 2005; and*

Whereas: *The O'Learys and CI Travel have supported several nonprofit programs in Hampton Roads, including several arts organizations and CANDII, and Mr. O'Leary is a primary creator of Old Dominion University's Port & Maritime Institute: and*

Whereas: *Richard & Barbara O'Leary are now retiring:*

Now, Therefore, I, Meyera E. Oberndorf, Mayor of the City of Virginia Beach, Virginia, do hereby Proclaim:

July 27, 2005
Richard & Barbara O'Leary Day

In Virginia Beach, and I call upon all citizens to extend their best wishes to this entrepreneurial team on the occasion of their retirement.

In Witness Whereof, I have hereunto set my hand and caused the Official Seal of the City of Virginia Beach, Virginia, to be affixed this Twenty-seventh day of July, Two Thousand Five.

Meyera E. Oberndorf

Meyera E. Oberndorf
Mayor

Above: RDO and Barbara at Fenway Park in Boston (a surprise birthday gift from Barbara).
Right: RDO and BBO skiing at Aspen.

Our family on our beach at low tide in Maine.

32

Our Family

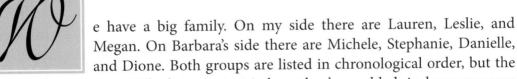e have a big family. On my side there are Lauren, Leslie, and Megan. On Barbara's side there are Michele, Stephanie, Danielle, and Dione. Both groups are listed in chronological order, but the order isn't important. What's important is how they've melded, in large measure because of Barbara's leadership and love.

There's a picture of the seven of them that I've shown to many visitors over the years and I've asked them to try to identify who belongs to whom. I think that's been accomplished only once. Look at the picture; I challenge you to try to answer the question.

Of great significance is the loving relationship that has developed among them. I don't mean a few; I mean all seven are like or even closer than blood sisters.

We also have twelve grandchildren. The picture on the following page was taken on the Fourth of July, 2010.

Top left, brothers Colin and Zachary. Top right, brothers Conner and Ryan. Brothers on each end, Skyler, in fifth grade, and Taylor, in first grade. Zachary is a senior in high school. Conner is a freshman in college. Donnie is in ninth grade. Jessica is in seventh grade. Morgan is in tenth grade. Kendall is in seventh grade. Colin is a sophomore in college, holding his baby brother, Christopher. Olivia is in kindergarten at age five. Kendall and Donnie are brother and sister.

In addition, we have two lovely goddaughters, Katie and Caroline Denton, who are now beautiful, accomplished women.

Almost all of them descend on us for four days and nights every Fourth of July in Ogunquit, Maine. Their mothers and an assortment of wonderful, interesting, and funny husbands or significant others also attend the festivities. This means that our house is overflowing with some twenty-five or thirty guests.

It's a gala event, enhanced for many years by spectacular fireworks on the beach in front of the house. A few years ago the show stopped because of plovers, small birds that were becoming extinct. Most of the younger children thought the fireworks were mine and questioned many times why I no longer had them. Thankfully, they've been reinstated.

Front row (left to right): Danielle Primack, who has two sons, created and co-owns a business that manufactures and sells Ultraleather. Stephanie Prettyman is a former television sales executive. She has three boys and a girl. Leslie Quisenberry, formerly sales manager of the Spirit of Washington, *has one daughter. Second row (left to right): Dione Boecker, a sales executive for an Internet and media company, has one daughter. Michele Heckman is a sales executive in the pharmaceutical industry. Lauren O'Leary is a sales executive for a realty company, and the mother of two boys. Megan Mayer, a former group manager of the* Spirit of Washington, *has a son and a daughter.*

One of the features of these visits has always been a major lobster bake, featuring loads of clams and lobsters cooked by Pop Pop (that's me).

The whole weekend is boisterous, and no one enjoys it more than Grammie, also known as Barbara. She calls it controlled chaos and loves every minute of it. For years, I used to say that it was all wonderful for about fifteen minutes, but I always had a great time, and I'm getting better.

As Barbara puts it, we have seven beautiful daughters on the outside and the inside and twelve terrific, healthy grandchildren plus three very beautiful and loving poodles. Her motto is that we are blessed, and she's right.

❧ 33 ❧

Famous Neighbors

he title of this chapter, especially the word "neighbors," is a bit of a stretch, but I like it. I mentioned in the introduction that we have a view from our home in Ogunquit of the wide-open Atlantic Ocean. If you turn your head a little to the left, you're looking across part of the Gulf of Maine at Kennebunkport. The distance is about twelve miles by land and six miles by water. By the way, Ogunquit is an Indian word meaning "beautiful place by the sea." Believe me, it is.

In addition to our Ogunquit home, located in the middle of the famous Marginal Way, we have a condominium on the harbor in Kennebunkport. It's a nice diversion for us and our poodles. We drive over there about once a week. One of the main reasons is that there we can take the dogs to the beach, which is permissible between five in the evening to nine in the morning. We can't do that in Ogunquit until after October 1.

As most people know, Kennebunkport is the home of George Herbert Walker Bush, the forty-first president of the United States, and his wife, Barbara. They live in a beautiful seaside house and are active members of the community.

They generously support all kinds of local activities. At one time, a long time ago, the president was the tennis pro at the Kennebunkport Tennis Club. A much more recent athletic event involved him skydiving out of a plane for his eighty-fifth birthday and landing on the lawn of St. Anne's Church, where the Bushes were married.

We're in our twenty-third year of living in these two wonderful towns. We've seen the Bushes many times: on the beach, in restaurants, and walking. We played golf right behind them and Millie the dog in the rain just after his unsuccessful bid for reelection.

There's a famous restaurant here in Ogunquit called Barnacle Billy's. The restaurant is in Perkins Cove, a little harbor filled with fishing boats. It has a wraparound porch that looks down on the picturesque cove. I've been going there for many years, long before we bought our house in Ogunquit. On especially beautiful days I'll say to Barbara, "Is this a dandelion day?" This phrase is from a Rod McKuen poem. If the answer is yes, we end up on the porch at Barnacle Billy's. Many of our out-of-town friends and family have also been there often.

Another family who enjoys the experience is the Bushes, along with their friends. However, they come across the six miles by boat. The former president drives a cigarette boat and is accompanied by escort Secret Service watercraft. Anyway, over the years we've seen them there many times. Consistent with their understated style, there's almost no fuss; they usually sit at a plain round lawn-type metal table in the corner. All the other diners, although excited, allow them their privacy.

Barbara and I never bother them other than to say hello. A few years ago, though, I was in the process of selling my seventy-five-foot Little Harbor sailboat, designed by the famous yachtsman Ted Hood, to Robert Mosbacher, who was President Bush's secretary of commerce. He has since passed away.

I left our table to do something and because the sale was in process, I approached President Bush and his wife, excused myself, and told them that I had recently spent the better part of two days with their friend.

They graciously insisted that I sit down. They already knew about the purchase and we had a lovely conversation. At the table was a Catholic priest with his collar on and a man in a cardigan sweater, who turned out to be Cardinal Law, of Boston. The only small problem was that once in a while I would see my Barbara signaling with her eyes for me to stop bothering them. In any case, they are wonderful, approachable people.

As I write this, it's now September 2010, and yesterday was a dandelion day, so we went to Billy's for lunch. The Bushes arrived about fifteen minutes later and we were one table away. Other than a little difficulty walking, the president

A postcard showing the Bush compound in Kennebunkport.

looked fit and youthful. Barbara Bush came by car, I think, probably because there were some pretty large swells from Hurricane Igor.

I expressed to my Barbara walking home what a perfect day it was: gorgeous weather, great food, and being in the presence of people we respect very much.

In fact, I believe that President Bush was the most experienced and qualified president of my lifetime. He was a war hero, having been shot down in World War II; a successful businessman in Texas; ambassador to China; director of the Central Intelligence Agency; president of the Republican National Committee; vice president of the United States under President Reagan; and, of course, president of the United States.

I also think he was the most effective president of my lifetime. He oversaw the collapse of the Soviet Union and the Berlin Wall and did so with grace. He didn't go to the wall but stayed quietly in the Oval Office in order not to embarrass Mr. Gorbachev.

In my judgment, he executed Desert Storm perfectly. He carried out the war basically without cost to us. It was paid for by the Kuwaitis and other countries, whose leaders he knew because of his vast experience. In my opinion, he then did exactly the right thing in limiting the war to driving Saddam Hussein out of Kuwait but not continuing on to Baghdad. America is fortunate to have had the services of such a man and we consider ourselves lucky to have been living in the same area as our famous neighbors.

Another famous person has a house in Kennebunkport. That person is Jane Morgan, the cabaret and Broadway star. Her name was Currier when she grew up in Kennebunkport and she worked at the local ice-cream shop. I believe at one time she held the record for most appearances on the Ed Sullivan television show. She also performed all over Europe.

I first saw her at the Persian Room at the Plaza Hotel in New York in the 1960s. The Persian Room was a very beautiful space with all the seats covered in handsome stripes. In those days she sang with a dozen violins. Her opening was a spectacular rendition of "Fascination." The Persian Room was on the left just as you walked in the Fifth Avenue entrance. Unfortunately it is no longer there.

Years later I saw her in Kennebunkport at her brother's small theater. She starred in one of the plays she had done on Broadway. When the play ended, she came out and sat on the edge of the stage and sang for about thirty minutes. She was wonderful and beautiful.

About five years ago I saw an ad for a fundraiser for her brother's work. He had passed away. It was to take place in a high school auditorium with a reception after at Blueberry Hill, her farm. The charge was nominal, something like twenty-five dollars. It was advertised as a Champagne Reception. I remember remarking to Barbara that it couldn't be much of a reception, probably a tiny sip of champagne out of a plastic cup!

The concert was wonderful. There were no violins but she was as great as ever. And I was wrong about the reception. It was fabulous. You entered through the barn where all her gowns and posters from Broadway were on display. The event for about 500 or so was staged under a tent and was splendid. The champagne and hors d'oeuvres were terrific.

We stood in a short receiving line, and when we reached her Barbara told her that I had been in love with her for many years. I was once again trying to find a place to hide.

The next day was another dandelion day and we were again at Barnacle Billy's! I told Billy about the evening and asked if he had seen her. He replied that she was in another section of the porch! On the way out we stopped at her table and Barbara told her how much we had enjoyed the evening. She looked up at me and said, "I remember you!" I walked home "With a Song in my Heart."

34

Postscript

The day after my retirement party was a Thursday, and I'd planned to use most of that day to wrap up the details. I went to my office and had a really busy morning producing a flurry of memorandums and signing and giving away my beautiful books to employees. Barbara and I were going to fly to Boston early the next morning.

There were a good number of people in the offices but the new executive team didn't come in. I was relieved and considered this an act of sensitivity by them.

For years it had been a practice to hold little parties for people's birthdays in a small coffee room near my office. I would usually be invited down and would attend for a couple of minutes but not sit down. A number of times I suggested that they have one celebration per month for all the birthday celebrants. This was said more in jest than seriously.

At about one o'clock, I was called over to the coffee room. I thought to myself that they were even going to do this on my last day. I caught on that this was different: it was for me. I was invited to sit, but I declined: "I don't want to break tradition," I said. This was a very sad scene. There were about twenty people in the room, and I think everyone cried. I didn't, but my heart was aching. I walked out realizing that it was really over and that soon I'd also be leaving my adopted city, one that had given me much happiness and success.

We flew away the next morning. I remember telling Barbara that I felt like I was deserting all those employees.

The next day I said I was feeling emotional and needed to do something. We had been going to buy a second standard poodle the previous Christmas and at the last moment changed our minds. Now I suggested we go do it right then. Barbara informed me that the breeder, who also ran a pet store, had decided to keep the dog. I explained to her that this didn't matter because this was America: I would take the steps necessary to see that he sold her to us. I was prepared to do what any good American who believed in capitalism would do—keep raising the price. We drove to Kennebunkport. We went to see the man but my plan didn't work; he loved the dog.

As preposterous as this may sound, we bought a condominium on the harbor instead. That's where I am as I write this. It's about six in the morning and Barbara is sleeping downstairs with our three standard poodles.

We left for our home in Ogunquit mid-morning. When we arrived, Barbara began to work at an annual ritual. We have a small plot of land, about fifteen by forty feet, in which she grows vegetables. It never produces much but it satisfies some need in her to show that she comes from Iowa. This year the job was complicated by the fact that our poodles had planted themselves in the three sections she had reserved for lettuce, tomatoes, and peppers. I think they liked the cool, damp soil, and it was difficult trying to persuade them to move.

As I look back at what I've written and the adventure writing has taken me on, I'm pleased that I undertook the challenge.

I've kept my word and not bothered the people at C.I. I did go back once to an annual company meeting when they named the Employee of the Year award after me.

Since I was very young, I've deeply loved all animals. I have recently made some donations that have been directed to that cause. I support shelters in four cities. One of them is called Friends of Gummi. Gummi was a dog who had no teeth. That shelter has become a major benefactor for cats in Naples, Florida. We're also the donors who rebuilt the Lobster Point Lighthouse in Ogunquit. This is a tourist attraction in the middle of the famous Marginal Way. It's not a real lighthouse but it faces the open Atlantic Ocean, looking northeast, and now it looks much more authentic.

Clockwise from top left: Genevieve Galliford, RDO, BBO, and Walter Galliford.

RDO, BBO, Lindy, Maureen, and Moe Ray.

Another thing that has been eating up my time and my net worth for the past five years involves trees. I planted some trees on my own land and a new neighbor in Maine, who actually lives in Pasadena, California, is suing me, claiming these plantings constitute a spite fence. Unbelievably, so far we are losing. For the second time in my life, the first being in Los Angeles, I believe we have encountered a prejudiced judge. But we are going to the Court of Appeals, so we shall see. In case some readers might conclude that I must be a litigious person, I have never sued anyone and have only been sued twice in business or personally.

Thankfully in retirement we have a good number of friends both in Maine and Florida. However, there is an old saying that old friends are the best friends. The two Moes, Maureen and Walter Ray, have brought us much pleasure for over twenty years, both in the north and the south.

Walter and Genevieve Galliford have been close friends for more than thirty-five years. With this couple you get a dividend. Genevieve is originally from Paris and she is a chanteuse, willing to sing in French at the end of dinner parties. I mentioned in the introduction that Walter was a scholarly gentleman. He is that, and also was the second-fastest runner in the world behind Jesse Owens while running for the University of Virginia.

Other old friends include Geraldine Nicholson and her late husband, Tommy, whose villa we visited twice in Italy. Jim and Bobi Eroncig have been our traveling and boating companions for many years. John and Claire Bertucci have added a new, very pleasurable chapter to our lives and introduced us to some new

RDO and friend Jim Denton.

cultural interests. And then there is the inimitable Parker Laite and his late wife, Reny, who entertained us and our friends many times in Camden, Maine, at their gorgeous lake house. I think it is probably obvious that Jodi and Bob Dickinson have been with us for many gala occasions through the decades, both in Maine and around the world.

I'm very pro-life. I used to be pro-choice but a bumper sticker converted me. It reads: "It's Not a Choice, It's a Life." My conversion is more dramatic than this suggests. I'm pro-life pertaining to everything: fish, insects, birds, you name it. I'm not fanatical, though; my philosophy is tempered with a little common sense and some moderation. I think some of this conversion is due to becoming more aware of my own mortality.

Life is good, and I'm working at being a bit of a recluse. Barbara hates the word and when I tell people that, she cringes. We live in Naples, Florida, in the winter. Recently we were having lunch with Jim Denton at a great restaurant called Sea Salt. There was a wonderful lunch special if you sat at the bar, so that's where we were. It was the day of the Kentucky Derby and I was talking to the bartender about making a bet. I was also engaged in a five-way conversation. There was a woman sitting next to us who had lost her house in the Madoff scandal. Also gathered around us were my favorite waiter and the charming owner of the restaurant, Fabrizio Aielli, who is from Italy; Venice, to be exact. You might say it was a bit of a three-ring circus. Jim Denton bent over to me and said quietly, "Another reclusive moment." But I'm trying.

When I decided to try to write this memoir, I immediately thought of my father, who was such a huge force in my life. I was going to entitle it *Son of Danny Boy* to make my story more fanciful and more Irish. Most of my father's work friends did call him Danny, but seldom Danny boy. That didn't matter to me. Every time I hear that song I'm engulfed by emotion and I think of how grand he was.

As I wrote, however, I realized that he died in 1974 and that many things happened to me after that event. That led to a reconsideration of the title. For that reason, and because he was truly the progenitor of all that transpired to make my life what it has been, I think it's appropriate to end with the beautiful lyrics from "Danny Boy."

Danny Boy

Oh, Danny Boy, the pipes, the pipes are calling
From glen to glen, and down the mountain side,
The summer's gone, and all the roses falling,
It's you, it's you must go and I must bide.
But come ye back when summer's in the meadow,
Or when the valley's hushed and white with snow,
It's I'll be here in sunshine or in shadow,
Oh, Danny Boy, oh, Danny Boy, I love you so!

But when ye come, and all the flowers are dying,
If I am dead, as dead I well may be,
Ye'll come and find the place where I am lying,
And kneel and say an Ave there for me;
And I shall hear, though soft you tread above me,
And all my grave will warmer, sweeter be,
For you will bend and tell me that you love me,
And I shall sleep in peace until you come to me!

View from Ogunquit home looking east.

Acknowledgments

tried to make it clear in the introduction that I knew virtually nothing about writing or putting a book together when I began this project. One of the first things I had to do was find a publisher. Some of my well-meaning, sophisticated friends thought it should be a large New York publisher and that I would need contacts and probably assistance from some sort of ghost writer or cowriter.

Since I was in Maine for the summer I looked in the Yellow Pages in the local areas. I found the name of Peter E. Randall Publisher in Portsmouth, New Hampshire.

I later learned that the company had been in business for over forty years. The founder is still active but his daughter Deidre, is now the CEO. Barbara and I met with her and learned about the company and examined some of the beautiful books they have produced. We were impressed, and the fact that she was encouraging, and was located about ten miles away, sold the deal for us. She and Leslie and the rest of her team were perfect for me and I have never regretted it for one moment. It has been a thoroughly enjoyable experience.

I next had the opportunity to have some very professional assistance. Again, through the aid of friends, I was introduced to a very experienced and professional writer. She was very busy but was willing to assist me. However, there first was a three-week delay, and then an unexpected four-month further delay before she could begin. I decided to continue on my own. So, to paraphrase an old expression, "What you read is what you get!" It is all mine.

I would be remiss if I did not mention Barbara Hoppe, who translated my scribblings from yellow notepads into something legible. Grace Peirce, who also teaches the Adobe® Creative Suite® software at the University of New Hampshire, is responsible for the cover and layout design. She is part of the Randall team and is also very gracious.

Jim Denton, an old colleague and now the editor and publisher of *World Affairs* journal in Washington, D.C., has been extraordinarily helpful, persistent, and encouraging. Jerome Daly, the Irish oral historian, has added much to my knowledge of Ireland and my father's early life. I also want to thank Tom Vincent for leading me to the title of this memoir.

I must thank Barbara for her love, patience, and invaluable assistance. She is the only person in the world who has heard every word of what I have written.

I use the word "heard" deliberately because of the routine I got into. I would start early in the morning, by five or six o'clock, and write for four or five hours, and then I would read it to her. She has also read the entire manuscript a number of times.

My daughters, without knowing much of the details of this project, were always encouraging, which helped me to stay the course.

About the same time I started this project I started making a few notes in a beautiful leather-bound book Barbara gave me for my birthday. I will end this section with a few comments from those writings:

"I know nothing about writing a memoir—nothing about style or syntax or anything. So what, I have started and it is not nearly as bad as I thought it would be."

On July 26, 2010, I wrote the following:

> There is a timeless Maritime tradition on ships. When the vessel returns to port and is tied up securely, an officer puts the Engine Order telegraph on F.W.E. —Finished with engines. It does not really shut the engines down but rather symbolically signals the engineering officer below to shut them down. I have just shut down my engines on this book project. It is finished except for clean up writing. Little did I know I would still be writing on it just before Thanksgiving. For something I never wanted to do, it was a blast.

About the Author

ichard O'Leary was born in Auburn, Maine, in 1932. He attended the Maine Maritime Academy in Castine, Maine, where he earned a bachelor of science degree. He later completed the Alexander Hamilton Institute's course in Modern Business. He went on to earn a masters in business administration from Adelphi University with a graduate tuition scholarship. He was also awarded an honorary doctor of science degree from the Maine Maritime Academy, and was one of the first twelve inductees into that institution's Wall of Fame.

He served in both the U.S. Navy and the U.S. Merchant Marine. He also was the Commandant of Midshipmen at the U.S. Merchant Marine Academy at Kings Point, New York.

He then moved to Norfolk, Virginia, and became the assistant general manager of the Norfolk Port and Industrial Authority. Three years later, in 1972, he founded a new company called Cruise Ventures, Inc., that did business as Cruise International and C.I. Travel. Mr. O'Leary retired in 2005 after thirty-four years as CEO and chairman of the board.

Mr. O'Leary has received a number of honors and awards in his career including being named by *Irish America* magazine as one of the one hundred top Irish business people in America.

He resides with his wife, Barbara, in Kennebunkport and Ogunquit, Maine, in the summer and Naples, Florida, in the winter.

Appendix

 have included a few of the letters I received for the memory book presented to me at my retirement celebration that are particularly important to me. I have also included some of the awards Cruise International/C.I. Travel received.

- Page 235: Letter from Ken Curtis, Governor of State of Maine, 1967–1975
- Page 236: John L Roper, III, former CEO, Norfolk Shipbuilding and Drydock Corp.
- Page 237: Letter from Dr. Mason C. Andrews, former mayor, City of Norfolk, Virginia
- Page 238: Letter from Federal Judge Robert Doumar
- Page 239: Letter from Charles E. Payne, former general counsel, Cruise International/C.I Travel Centers
- Page 240: Letter from Robert E. Hart, chairman, 1988 Maritime Day and World Trade Week, Port of New York and New Jersey
- Page 241-244: Awards earned by Cruise International/C.I. Travel

STATE OF MAINE
OFFICE OF THE GOVERNOR
AUGUSTA, MAINE
04330

KENNETH M. CURTIS
GOVERNOR

Dear Richard:

Congratulations on your retirement. However, knowing you, I expect that you will be busier than ever. At any rate, accept my best wishes for many more years of good health and happiness.

During our longtime friendship we have shared many good times. We do go back many years. In fact, we were close at birth, having been born in Androscoggin county, Maine, eighteen miles apart. I expect that growing up by the Androscoggin River downwind from one of Maine's famous paper mills was the inspiration for your love of the sea.

I enjoyed being an upperclassman when you entered Maine Maritime Academy as a "Midshipman under guidance." Boy, you could shine shoes better than any other "mug" on C Deck!

We enjoyed many laughs when Polly and I left St. Thomas and you stood on the deck shouting for all yachtsmen to hear. "And don't come back!"

Richard, you have enjoyed many successes and make all of us from Maine very proud. However, your crowning achievement surely was conning Barbara into becoming Mrs. O'Leary.

All the best, your lifelong friend,

Ken Curtis

JOHN L. ROPER, III
207 GRANBY STREET, SUITE 303
NORFOLK, VA 23510
757-622-7790

April 28, 2005

Mr. Richard D. O'Leary , Chairman
C. I. Travel Cruise International
800 World Trade Center
Norfolk, VA 23510

Dear Richard:

So you are retiring. What is it that the say about old sailors never retiring - they just get a little dinghy!!! Somehow a "little dinghy" and "O'Leary" just don't go together — in more ways than one.

We go back so far and have so many memories - and at my age, while memories may be all I have, they are getting harder and harder to recall. But I do remember fondly those first days of the *Spirit* boats and especially the one with at least fourteen reverse pitch propellers - none of which worked. If your paying passengers ever looked over the other side they would have seen the Norshipco tug "George W. Roper" (named for my grandfather and NOT my brother) providing the forward motion!!!

And all those wonderful visits to Maine. Poor Jinnie. Will she ever get over her seasickness! And will she ever forgive us. And Naples!! If you keep buying bigger boats, they will have to pull the *S.S. United States* out of dry dock for you.

Richard, I am glad to have known you these many years. You have been a great business partner, traveling companion, and most of all, wonderful friend. You have made me a lot of money and I hope that I have been able to give you some sound advice over the years. I do know that the second best thing you ever did (on my advice) was to make Barbara a Director; the first was to marry her!!

Congratulations on your retirement. You deserve it!!

With best personal regards,

Sincerely

Eastern Virginia Medical School
Department of Obstetrics and Gynecology

The Howard and Georgeanna Jones
Institute for Reproductive Medicine

EASTERN VIRGINIA
MEDICAL SCHOOL

November 16, 1996

Dear Dick and Barbara:

You are the most! Sabine and I deeply appreciate your extreme kindness and thoughtfulness to us on Friday.

The whole event had monumental proportions beyond the obvious reasons as a present and future benefit to our area and as a dramatization of what a difference individuals can make through the free enterprise system, through vision and sound management to produce and sell a better product (in this case the Spirit Cruises, the cruise business and the travel business).

In the process, you helped the Carnival owners to succeed and, as a byproduct, caused the historic event of Friday with its many beneficial consequence now and in the future.

Furthermore; stopping to recognize and do a favor for ones you had met along the way displays qualities which I enjoy encountering in various successful people and which nourish my idealism.

For this reason, the specialness of Friday recalls a few other special experiences in our lives involving fine people such as: - being Jim Rouse's only guests at the opening ceremonies at Harbor Place in Baltimore; riding up the Hudson on Steve Forbes' "Highlander" with one hundred really distinguished guests; being guests at a dinner given by the President of Princeton honoring Berry Brazelton (child development guru and longtime friend); and such as Howard Jones making me a partner in producing and announcing the first invitro baby in the United States.

Sincerly,

Mason

Mason C. Andrews

In VItro Fertilization • Gift • Tubal Surgery . Microsurgery • Laser Surgery • Ovulation Induction • Male Infertility (Andrology)
• Sperm Bank • Contraception • Menstrual Irregularities • Hirsutism • Congenital Anomalies • Menopause

Contributed by Mason C. Andrews, former Mayor of Norfolk, VA

Dick O'Leary is part of the genesis of the New Norfolk which has emerged during the last 25 years.

He has developed two thriving businesses which are important to the region, and he is very good company and a sound advisor and citizen participant when he stays long enough to catch him.

He drew on his experience as navigation officer of the **S.S. United States** to postulate that a dinner cruise in Hampton Roads harbor might give some of the same pleasure experienced by the more affluent on the **United States**. His first attempt with a converted LCI ran into various problems including a running adversarial relationship with the city manager's office. They don't teach about dinner cruises in city manager school. I hope I was of some help during that time.

The Spirit Cruises flourished in Norfolk and many other cities, were sold, and continue to enhance the tourist business and options for recreation and entertainment in Norfolk.

His prior experience led him to found Cruise International/CI Travel which he and Barbara have developed into the 31st largest travel company in the United States. In the early days some problems had to be fixed there also. One summer morning I was having breakfast on our boat at the Tides Inn dock when someone came running from the Tides Inn saying that someone wanted to talk to me. It was Dick O'Leary who was having some kind of trouble in parking passengers at Norfolk International terminals. I don't remember what the problem was or why I could help. But with Dick's persistence and skill, that and many other problems were surmounted.

Any reference to the O'Leary contribution to the quality of life in our area must report that Barbara was an important part of the team as she has always made the world more beautiful. Furthermore, she has helped many others to do so. For many years, as I made morning rounds in the hospital, all the TV sets were tuned to Barbara showing them the proper exercises. These looked pretty good to the doctor too.

I'm sorry that Dick and Barbara are retiring and wish them all satisfactions. I hope they will stay here enough and continue to contribute to the quality of life with their company and their brains.

United States District Court
Eastern District of Virginia
Norfolk, Virginia 23510

Chambers of
Robert G. Doumar
District Judge

Walter E. Hoffman U. S. Courthouse
600 Granby Street

December 14, 2004

Dear Barbara:

Richard has achieved so much in so short a time as to be astounding. From the Merchant Marine Academy, which he headed, to the **S.S. United States** to the accomplishments of Cruise International, he never once thought small, but always progressed forward. He never sought personal aggrandizement but always was most considerate of others. When approached by a group of Republican leaders to run for the state legislature with the Republican nomination assured by the group, he declined as he felt he was better able to help his fellow man by utilizing his efforts and money to help the more deprived and to use his influence to persuade those in office to do what was best for the community.

As the founder and head of Cruise International, one of the largest travel company's in the United States, he has constantly strived to empathize that which was most beneficial, not only to his own employees, but to the public at large.

Yours truly,

Robert G. Doumar

CHARLES E. PAYNE
ATTORNEY AND COUNSELOR AT LAW
3357 Herons Gate
Virginia Beach, Virginia 23452
(757) 431-0300
FAX (757) 431-2618
cpayne@q-express.net

Corporate Law & Finance
Intellectual Property Law
Civil Litigation

Of Counsel To:
Payne, Gates, Farthing
& Radd, P.C.

999 Waterside Drive. Suite 1500 Norfolk,
Virginia 23510-3309

(757) 640-1500; Fax (757) 627-6583
cpayne@q-express.

April 1, 2004

Richard D. O'Leary,
Chairman and CEO Cruise International/CI Travel
101 W. Main Street, Ste 800
Norfolk, Va. 23510

Re: Milestones

Dear Richard:

It goes without saying that a milestone of great import has been reached in the life of the company and your personal life as well. As is your custom, you carefully thought out and planned these changes well in advance. The result has been to attain the best succession with the minimum disruption. The way you have handled it is a model that many other business owners could benefit from emulating, because it shows deep, genuine concern for the future of the company and its owners, both original and new.

As I have looked back and tried to grasp the essence of your leadership during all the years that have passed since you first formed the company, it may be summarized as bold vision, high standards, and a keen sense of duty to those who placed their trust in you.

Congratulations to you, Richard, for your achievement and the remarkable legacy you leave: a legacy of ownership to your employees, of wealth to your investors, and far more valuable, a legacy of learning to all who have been engaged with you in this enterprise.

With sincerest best wishes for your continued success, health, happiness and good fortune, I remain.

Cordially yours,

Chuck

MARINE INDEX BUREAU, INC.
1 7 BATTERY PLACE
NEW YORK, N.Y. 10004-]283

Telephone: 112-169-1100 Teletype
710-581-6111 Telex: 11-5139 Cable
Address: INDEXMARIN

30 May 1988

Richard D. O'Leary, President Cruise International / CI Travel Centers
501 Front Street, Norfolk, Virginia 23510

Dear Mr. O'Leary:

Thank you Richard...for being aboard and hosting our 1988 New York Maritime Day program. You and Barbara were so kind to fly away from your busy schedule in the Norfolk area and join with us in the New York Port.

The City, the Port Authority and all those in the Shipping family of this area, appreciate your being with us, both ashore and afloat as we dedicated this year's observance to those Mariners who served in World War II.

On behalf of my great Maritime Day committee who did all the detailed work that made our day so successful, I send thanks and a few pix of the great day for your personal memoir book.

I would like to also state for the record, that the services performed by your NY Sales Director, Dom DeFilippi who served on our Committee was simply just outstanding. His expertise in coordinating the great SPIRIT OF NEW YORK and our detailed program including the execution from planning stage through the final hour was the best I have observed since I have been Chairman for the past twenty years. We are proud and you should be informed of this fine performance of one of your own people.

In the meantime, all best regards and 'Thanks Again!', and without your support from Cruise International our most successful Maritime Day program could not have been possible.

Jane joins me in best wishes to both you and Barbara.

Most Sincerely,

Robert E. Hart
Chairman, 1988 Maritime Day
and World Trade Week, Port of
New York and New Jersey

Awards

.I. Travel, the leisure, commercial, and government travel divisions of Cruise Ventures, Inc., as of January 8, 2010, has earned the following business awards and commendations:

1984: Received a five-year contract from the General Services Administration to service more than $1,500,000 annual air sales for all non-DOD agencies in the Norfolk area. C.I. Travel was the first agency in southeastern Virginia to service the government. This contract was revamped in 1989 as a small business set-aside.

1985: Entered into a memorandum of understanding (MOU) with NATA SACLANT, an account that has grown to $5,500,000 annually and is still serviced by C.I. Travel twenty-five years later.

1987: Awarded a two-year contract by the U.S. Air Force at Langley Air Force Base, Hampton, Virginia, to service $8,000,000 in annual official and unofficial travel. C.I. Travel opened three offices just for this account. Langley was the first contract awarded by DOD in southeastern Virginia.

1989: Awarded a second contract for four years by Langley AFB. Volume had grown to approximately $9,000,000.

1992: Awarded a five-year contract by Patrick Air Force Base and Cape Canaveral Air Force Station. C.I. Travel opened three on-site locations to service the annual volume of $5,800,000. At renewal time, this contract was set aside for small business.

1993: Awarded a third contract for five years by Langley AFB. At this time, volume was approximately $12,500,000. The contract included Seymour Johnson Air Force Base, in Goldsboro, North Carolina, an account with an annual volume of approximately $1,500,000. In 2002, the Langley/Seymour Johnson contract was set aside for small business. C.I. Travel continued to serve this account as a subcontractor until its award to The Alamo Travel Group, in 2005, as part of the Defense Travel Service Small Business Set-Aside contract.

1995:   Awarded a five-year contract by Wright-Patterson Air Force Base, Dayton, Ohio. C.I. Travel opened six locations to service this account. The original volume was approximately $35,000,000 annually.

1996:   Awarded a five-year, $8,500,000-a-year contract by the U.S. Navy to provide leisure travel service for all Norfolk-area naval installations on behalf of the Morale Welfare and Recreation Department. C.I. Travel opened nine locations to serve this account.

1996:   Commended by the U.S. State Department and Commander, Air Force Materiel Command, for work in support of travel needs at the Bosnian Peace Conference, which was held in Dayton, Ohio.

1997:   Awarded the Society of Travel Agents in Government (now the Society of Government Travel Professionals, SGTP) award for Best Travel Agency Program–Government.

2000:   Awarded a four-year, $90,000,000 contract by NASA to provide official travel service for eleven NASA centers nationwide and leisure travel services for Kennedy Space Center, Florida. To service this contract, C.I. Travel opened nine locations and subcontracted two. In addition, a central reservation center (CRC), dedicated to NASA, was established in our Norfolk corporate/government operations center.

2000:   Awarded our second Society of Travel Agents in Government award for Best Travel Agency Program–Government.

2000:   Awarded a five-year U.S. Coast Guard Engineering Logistics Center contract, Task Order number GS-09F-80756.

2000:   Awarded a second five-year contract by the U.S. Navy Exchange Service to provide leisure travel service for all Norfolk-area installations on behalf of the Morale Welfare and Recreation (MWR) Department.

2001:   Awarded a second seven-year contract by Wright-Patterson AFB as a subcontractor to TECOM, the prime contractor, which received the award of a consolidated service contract, including official travel for the base

2001:   C.I. Travel's Joseph S. Good elected vice president of SGTP.

2001:   Awarded a third SGTP award for Best Travel Agent Program–Government.

2002:   C.I. Travel's Joseph S. Good received the SGTP Person of the Year award.

2003: Received a letter of appreciation from NASA for "Responsiveness to the Columbia Shuttle Accident."

2003: Received a letter of commendation from Admiral Gehman, Columbia Accident Investigation Board (CAIB) director, for "Outstanding Support to the Columbia Accident Investigation Board."

2004: Awarded our fourth SGTP award for Best Travel Agency Program–Government.

2005: Awarded a five-year contract to continue serving NASA headquarters and its eleven Space and Research Centers. This was the first time in NASA history that an incumbent travel management center (TMC) was awarded a follow-on contract.

2005: Awarded a two-year contract with the U.S. Securities and Exchange Commission.

2005: Awarded a fifth SGTP award for Best Travel Agency Program–Government.

2005: Kevin J. McElroy, C.I. Travel's president, elected to the board of SGTP.

2006: Awarded a follow-on, one-year contract with the SEC.

2007: Awarded a sixth SGTP award for Best Travel Agency Program–Government.

2008: Awarded a five-year contract for DHS USCIS.

Special Travel Awards earned by C.I. Travel

- Top 30 Corporate Travel Agencies, *Business Travel News* (since 2000)
- Power List of Agencies, *Travel Weekly* (2004)
- Top 50 U.S. Travel Agencies, *Business Travel News*
- Top 50 U.S. Travel Agencies, *Travel Weekly* (since 2000)
- Best Travel Agency, *Virginian Pilot* Reader's Poll (multiple years in multiple cities)
- Best Travel Agency, *Daily Press* Reader's Choice Awards (2006)
- Best Travel Agency, *Hampton Roads Monthly* Reader's Choice (2004)
- Top Producer Award, Celebrity Cruises/Royal Caribbean
- Winner's Circle Award, Carnival Cruise Lines
- Multiple awards for Best Travel Agency in Government, Society of Government Travel Professionals

- Multiple "Professional Development" awards, Society of Government Travel Professionals
- Wright-Patterson Air Force Base letter of commendation for role in assisting travel arrangements during the Balkan peace talks
- NASA letter of recognition from the Columbia Accident Investigation Board for assistance during the review of the Columbia Shuttle accident
- Wright-Patterson Air Force Base letter of appreciation for outstanding support in the implementation of the electronic Defense Travel System (DTS)
- NASA certificate of appreciation for exceptional dedication, hard work, and expertise in support of the Return to Flight Task Force for the Columbia Shuttle

Index